Merry Christmas! to Grandma and Grandad-
We love you, and hop
Bro. Petersen's book.

Love,
Bob, Kristi & Judd
Christmas 1976

◊ THE SALT
AND THE
SAVOR

THE SALT AND THE SAVOR

MARK E. PETERSEN

BOOKCRAFT, INC.
Salt Lake City, Utah

Copyright © 1976 by Bookcraft, Inc.

Library of Congress Catalog Card Number: 76-26436
ISBN 0-88494-306-2

First Printing, 1976

Lithographed in the United States of America
PUBLISHERS PRESS
Salt Lake City, Utah

FOREWORD

"Ye are the salt of the earth: but if the salt have lost his savour, wherewith shall it be salted? it is thenceforth good for nothing, but to be cast out, and to be trodden under foot of men." (Matthew 5:13.)

This warning given by the Savior early in his great Sermon on the Mount runs as a golden thread through the pattern of Elder Mark E. Petersen's timely messages. Not only opportune in meeting head-on the problems of the day, they are also replete with the wise counsel, admonition, forthrightness and clarity with which this modern-day apostle and crusader for righteousness has long been identified.

Every message herein presented purposely helps mark the pathway by which the faithful followers of the Savior may indeed become "the salt of the earth" and "the light of the world" whose light shines forth with good works to glorify their "Father which is in heaven." (Matthew 5:14-16.)

This volume adds yet another to the several books by Elder Petersen containing selected editorials appearing weekly as a popular feature of the *Church News,* a section of the *Deseret News.* For more than three decades this beloved member of the Council of the Twelve of The Church of Jesus Christ of Latter-day Saints has authored these editorials. His inspired, crusading voice is well worth listening to.

HENRY A. SMITH

CONTENTS

Salt and Savor, Sheep and Goats 1

1. CHURCH AND KINGDOM

Going "Church-Shopping" 7
Of Greatest Worth 8
Vitality in Religion 10
Living for Today 11
It Is Verily True 12
The Good Shepherd 13
Our Rapid Expansion 15
The Worldwide Church 15
What July Twenty-fourth Means 17
When We Say "Amen" 18
The Lines Are Drawn 19

2. PROPHETS AND REVELATION

Dead Men Tell Tales 23
The Basic Principle 24
Stand By Your Chief 25
President's Authority 27
Follow the President 29
The Men Who Guide Us 30
The Spirit of Prophecy 31
The Lord's Warning 32
Yes, We Believe 34
The Right to Speak 35
Prophecy Fulfilled 37
Hear Ye Him! 38
Life and Resurrection 40
Immortality Is Real 41

3. DILIGENCE AND DEVOTION

He Expects Devotion 45
That Clear Signal 46
Faith and Faith Alone? 47
"Thinketh No Evil" 49
Salvation by Compromise? 50
Be Good and Do Good 50
Kindness Is the Key 52
Setting of Priorities 53
Can We Be Perfect? 54
A Guiding Light 55
The Drop-outs 56
"Add to Your Faith" 58
We Must Exercise It? 59
Preparation Needed 59
The Time to Act 61

4. LAW AND OBEDIENCE

Let Us Practice It 65
The Value of Laws 66
Reaping the Whirlwind 67
Correct Principles 68
Doing unto Others 70
For Our Security 71
Days of Violence 73
The Ten Commandments 74
"This Is the Law" 75
Full or Part Obedience? 76
Freedom of Religion 77
Godlessness Versus Liberty 78
Our Sunday Habits 79
The Lord's Frankness 80
Walking with God 81

5. SIN AND SOCIETY

A Permissive Society 85
The Evil of Vulgarity 86
How Great Is That Sin 87
Cure by Surrender? 88
Out of Sight and Mind 90
Is "Porno" a Disease? 92
A Moral Principle 93
The Sanctity of Life 95
The Silent Majority 96
That Unborn Life 98
On Limiting Families 99
Another Warning 100

6. HONESTY AND INTEGRITY

Christianity and Honesty 105
A Way of Life — Really? 106
The Need of Business 107
Dishonesty Is Fatal 108
Honest Work, Honest Pay 109
Good Checks and Bad 110
Public Honesty 111
Immorality in High Places 112
Games of Chance 114
Cost of Gambling 115
Work Not in Darkness 116
As We Mete to Others 117

7. KNOWLEDGE AND WISDOM

How Shall We Choose? 121
Faith and Knowledge 122
Teaching the Truth 123
Strength in Simplicity 124
The Scripture Search 125

We Need to Know 127
What Scriptures Teach 128
Our Eternal Identity 130
Our Sacred Scripture 131
What Saves a Nation? 133
To Replace Prayer 134
The Right to Disagree 136

8. WOMANHOOD AND MOTHERHOOD

The Child's Anchor 141
The Nobility of Women 142
Honor and Responsibility 143
Mother's Holy Calling 144
A Mother's Day Goal 145
Where Obligation Stops 147
Weighing the Values 148
When Mothers Work 150
Preserving Femininity 150
Equal Rights Amendment 152
Families Will Survive 154

9. MARRIAGE AND FAMILY

The Real Teachers 157
Our Learning Process 159
Having a Family 160
Like Father, Like Son 161
Home and Family 162
Fidelity Begets Fidelity 164
Those Broken Homes 165
Divorce Insurance 167
The Head of the Family 167
"I Love Him Best . . ." 168
Virtue in the Home 169
To Form or to Reform? 171
Where Delinquency Starts 173

10. CHILDREN AND YOUTH

Youth in Perspective 177
A Child Needs Love 178
Cuddling Children 179
The Child Victim 181
Children's Rights 181
Teaching Our Children 183
Teach Children Tithing 184
Pitfalls of Early Marriage 185
When Parents Weep 186
What Next? 188
Saving Our Youth 189
The Noble Birthright 190

11. HEALTH AND HAPPINESS

We Barter Survival! 195
Liquor or Famine 196
The Very First Drink 198
The Last Drink 199
Those Strong Drinks 199
Parental "Pushers" 201
Reforming Alcoholics 202
That Liquor Taste 204
The Suicide Rates 205
Teen Girl Smokers 206
How Coffee Hurts 207
Coffee and Your Heart 208
Coffee and Unborn Babes 209
Quashing the Killers 210
The Word of Wisdom 211

SALT AND SAVOR, SHEEP AND GOATS

Freedom is the watchword of today! Liberty, human rights, the privilege of self-determination, all of these are wrapped up in that one thrilling word — *freedom*.

As we celebrated the great American anniversary, the importance of freedom was impressed upon us more than ever. True freedom means life, joy and progress. Its loss means slavery.

It is no wonder that Patrick Henry declared: "Give me liberty or give me death."

But true liberty cannot be separated from God, for he is its Author. Does not the Bible declare the gospel to be the perfect law of liberty? (James 1:25.) The Book of Mormon is equally explicit in saying that the Spirit of God is the spirit of freedom. (Alma 61:15.)

We cannot separate freedom from Deity, for true freedom comes from no other source. Hence the necessity of living close to the Lord. This he expects of us. We must either be wholeheartedly for him or we are classed with those who are against him. Said the Lord:

"He that is not with me is against me; and he that gathereth not with me scattereth abroad." (Matthew 12:30.)

That principle divides the good from the bad, the obedient from the careless and disobedient. It determines whether we are true followers of the Lord or whether we drift away from him, even if only in neglect.

God has given to every person the full right of choice, that each one may act "according to the moral agency which I have given unto him, that every man may be accountable for his own sins in the day of judgment." (D&C 101:78.)

He gives us this agency so that we may choose our own way, chart our own course, plow our own furrow, and thus develop our own character traits.

We are living in crucial times, in the midst of such great challenges that now if ever we must stand up and be counted.

Never in our time has worldliness asserted itself so forcefully. Seldom has there been such a concerted effort to destroy all that is good, and to wipe out the standards, ideals and practices which in the past have made for strong character, sound families, and wholesome communities.

Indifference is one of our worst enemies — often our own indifference. How many are taking the "I-don't-care" attitude? How many say, "It can't happen to me"?

So completely do we "see through a glass darkly" that Satan takes advantage of the darkness which blinds us, and with false lights and a seductive voice, leads us on the way to destruction.

Where do we stand?

Are we firm in the faith?

Do we compromise with evil?

Are we halfhearted in our worship?

Do we obey only with reservations?

Are we hypocritical?

Let us examine ourselves, determine where we stand, and see in what direction we are facing. Unless we take a stand for the right, we may be engulfed in a flood of destruction.

To his modern saints, the Lord said that if we are not *valiant* in the faith, we shall lose the crown over the kingdom, and be barred from celestial glory. (D&C 76:79.)

When he spoke to his saints anciently he called them the salt of the earth, but warned them against losing their "savor." Said he:

"Ye are the salt of the earth: but if the salt have lost his savour, wherewith shall it be salted? it is thenceforth good for nothing, but to be cast out, and to be trodden under foot of men." (Matthew 5:13.)

Savor is at least as important to the Lord as it is to us. Certainly it means a great deal to human beings. Is there anyone who fails to appreciate good taste in food, as well as in other things? Is it not salt that gives the savor to food?

In ancient times as the people were taught to offer sacrifices on the altar, the prophets pointed out that the Lord appreciates the sweet savor of a proper offering. (Exodus 29:18.)

He also said that when he gathers his people in the latter days, he will accept them for "their sweet savor" and will sanctify them. (Ezekiel 20:41.)

Savor is important to God because it is a measure of the attitude of his people toward him. When there has been a savor "that stinketh," he has been greatly displeased (Joel 2:20), but when the savor is sweet, he pours out his blessings. And the degree of obedience displayed by the people is what determines the acceptability of the offering.

Every follower of Christ should regard himself as the salt of the earth and the savor of men. As the salt of the earth, his followers are intended to lend a sweet savor to mankind by teaching them — particularly through example — to live the gospel of Christ so that they also may become as salt, ready to sweeten the lives of others and give savor to them.

But when the salt has lost its savor, the Lord has said that it becomes of no value to him, and is fit only to be discarded. If we are the Lord's salt, dare we lose our savor?

How do we lose our savor in the eyes of God? It is only by disobedience, which can come a little at a time, so gradually that we hardly realize what is happening.

If we become careless about attending our meetings, do we not lose some of our savor?

If we neglect our prayers and our tithes and our offerings, what becomes of our savor?

If we are dishonest, unkind, or vengeful, do we not severely offend the Deity?

And if we lose our virtue — that priceless gift of chastity which God has given to each one of us — what becomes of our savor? Is not cleanliness next to godliness? Does not filth banish purity? Does not unchastity insult the Lord? Is it not a "savor that stinketh"?

If we oppose Church policies and leaders, and indulge in criticisms, what becomes of our "sweet savor"? Can there be any sweetness in disloyalty?

If we withdraw from the Church, and accept false teachings of false prophets, do we not abdicate our place in the Lord's house? How unfortunate are those who do not realize that there is salvation only in the Church, not in splinter groups!

We are the salt of the earth only if we follow the Lord and his true servants. To lose our savor can mean only one thing — to lose our salvation also.

The Lord meant business when he said: "He that is compelled in all things, the same is a slothful and not a wise servant; wherefore he receiveth no reward.

"Verily I say, men should be anxiously engaged in a good cause, and do many things of their own free will, and bring to pass much righteousness;

"For the power is in them wherein they are agents unto themselves. And inasmuch as men do good they shall in nowise lose their reward.

"But he that doeth not anything until he is commanded, and receiveth a commandment with a doubtful heart, and keepeth it with slothfulness, the same is damned." (D&C 58:26-29.)

We must take the Lord's word at face value. When he commands us to serve him with all our heart, might, mind and strength, we must know that he means what he says. And when he adds, "He that is slothful shall not be counted worthy to stand," we must understand that that is precisely what he means. (D&C 107:100.)

Can we misinterpret his description of the judgment day as given in Matthew, chapter 25? Surely we must know that as we do unto others, we shall be done by, for as we sow, in like measure shall we reap at the last day.

1.

CHURCH

AND

KINGDOM

GOING "CHURCH-SHOPPING"

A clergyman in Anaheim, California, addressed a congregation in his newly erected church building, and warned the people that they should not go "shopping around" from one church to another to see which they liked best. He urged that they content themselves with their own denomination without constantly looking for "greener pastures."

A clergyman in a smaller community resisted the granting of a building permit to Latter-day Saints who wished to build a chapel of their own in that town. His comment was: "We have enough churches here already. We don't need any more."

This indicated the obvious feeling that any church will lead to heaven, and that one is as good as another. But will any church save a soul? Is every church acceptable to God? If not, which is the right one? Can we find the true church among the hundreds of conflicting denominations without "shopping around," and without searching for the truth?

All roads do not lead to Rome, and all churches, with their confusion of conflicting creeds, do not lead to heaven. But since there are so many different denominations to choose from, which church should a person join if he is serious about his soul's salvation?

The Savior organized only one church. As he did so, he also taught that man-made creeds have no power to save and that worship by "the doctrines of man" is in vain. (Matthew 15.)

Then should not earnest souls "shop around" and actively seek the truth? How else may the truth be found? Certainly the various denominations do much good, and their creeds have many uplifting and ethical teachings. But do they always reflect Christ's doctrines? The Savior taught that man's ways are not necessarily God's ways. People can be sincere and yet mistaken.

Because nearly twenty centuries have elapsed since the Savior's mortal ministry, most Christians have only the Bible on which to rely. But properly read, it can be an unerring guide.

It points clearly to the unmistakable marks of identification of Christ's original church, with its living prophets, apostles, current revelation, a constantly growing body of scripture resulting from those revelations, and the power of the Holy Ghost being made manifest through men called to the ministry as was Aaron, by a living prophet. (Hebrews 5:4.)

The Savior urged us to "search the scriptures" to find the way of life (John 5:39), and yet Peter said that the scripture is not subject to private interpretation. (2 Peter 1:20.) It must be read in the light and context of other scripture for a proper understanding.

Everyone owes it to himself to find Christ's truth and, finding it, to hold fast to it.

OF GREATEST WORTH

What means most to us in life?

Is it family?

Is it church?

Is it pleasure?

Is it prestige?

Is it a good job or a career?

Is it a desire to make a contribution, either to the world at large or to individuals?

Is it to make a mark for ourselves, a reputation?

Is it to feed a sense of ego within us, and to prove that we can do things; that we are somebody; that we are deserving of the attention and admiration of others?

It is interesting to consider what the Lord regards as the most worthwhile thing in life. Repeatedly, in the early revelations of our time, he stressed that which is of most worth. Said he: "And now, behold, I say unto you, that the thing which will be of the most worth unto you will be to declare repentance unto this people, that you may bring souls unto me, that you may rest with them in the kingdom of my Father." (D&C 15:6; 16:6.)

The Lord looks at life in its eternal sense. Most of us look at it in a strictly temporal way, and many only as a day-to-day matter, but the Lord's is the only true point of view, and that we should accept.

We are eternal beings. We agree that mortality is but a short span in our everlasting existence, so the thing which is of most worth to us, of necessity, must be that which has eternal significance. That brings us directly to the Lord's point of view.

Only in blindness will we shut out the eternal nature of our careers. To look at today and only today, to look at the mortal and only the mortal, is to walk in darkness at midday.

Since we have the gospel, we must let it guide our lives and shape our destinies. Of course we must work for a living, and of course "man is that he might have joy," which includes good recreation, and of course we must have education, for "no man can be saved in ignorance."

But no one of those things should dominate our lives and shut out the rest. All should be placed in proper perspective, and made a part of the eternal program that God provides for our ultimate well-being.

To accept his word, realizing that in very deed the thing which is of most worth to us is his plan of salvation, is our only wise course.

"Seek ye first the kingdom of God and his righteousness"; "Declare repentance unto this people"; and "Bring souls unto me" — these should be the great goals of our lives.

To do this we must devote ourselves to the Church, keep the commandments, save ourselves and our families, and remember that we are our brothers' keepers and must be missionaries among those with whom we associate.

God's way is the only way to happiness and success.

VITALITY IN RELIGION

"Sacrifice brings forth the blessings of heaven." "Permissiveness sounds the death-knell of the denominations."

These two truisms were emphasized in a radio interview conducted over the Mutual Broadcasting System.

Featured was the Reverend Dean M. Kelley of the United Methodist Church, who gave reasons why the "old line" denominations are rapidly declining in membership while newer and more vigorous churches are moving rapidly ahead.

He indicated that the cause of the decline in churches of long standing is the tendency to give people whatever they want; in other words, surrendering to permissiveness.

The reason for growth in the progressive groups was explained as being the requirements made of their members by those churches, requirements of devotion, sacrifice and adherence to strict standards of conduct.

Said Mr. Kelley in this radiocast: "The fastest-growing church with over a million members is the Mormon Church, with headquarters in Salt Lake City, which is growing at the rate of 5 percent a year. That is a very rapid increase.

"The rapidly growing churches ask a great deal. For instance, the Mormons require that you spend two years as a missionary at your own expense. Now that is pretty serious."

Mr. Kelley went on to say that "the churches should quit being so sensitive to what outsiders think of them," and he urged that they hold to the high standards that have made the Christian religion a moving force in the past.

It is all reminiscent of what the Savior himself said. We cannot serve two masters; we cannot compromise with sin. "He that hath my commandments, and keepeth them, he it is that loveth me." (John 14:21.)

He also taught that if need be, we should even leave father or mother for his cause. Nor can we forget that the Master taught us to "seek first the kingdom of God and his righteousness." This certainly means sacrifice of worldliness.

The Prophet Joseph Smith said that "if we achieve celestial glory we must live the celestial law, and the whole law too."

Indeed, sacrifice brings forth the blessings of heaven, and surely permissiveness is but a surrender to the adversary.

Is it any wonder that our leaders continually urge us to "keep the commandments," and is it not this kind of obedience which has made our church the fastest growing one in the land?

LIVING FOR TODAY

Latter-day Saints, of all people, should live for today. The past is wonderful, the future is largely a mystery, but we do have today clearly in focus, filled with the new knowledge that comes constantly from various sources, and having all of the conveniences which now make life so easy.

But living for today, so far as we are concerned, must also mean that we will live in the light of today's truth, not merely the scientific knowledge which allows men to fight diseases with new medicines, or fly to the moon, or race in fast motor cars.

The true light for today is the light of modern revelation, which is given to us as a result of the restoration of the gospel. Living for today must mean living in the light of those modern revelations and the purpose for which they were given.

God has spoken in our day. He has given us a great purpose in life. He has called us to a special mission, to help prepare for the second coming of the Lord. What are we doing about it? How do we use our time?

Are we merely fitting into the routine of the rest of the world, playing, working, visiting, socializing? Or are we putting our time and effort into productive lines which not only will prepare us to meet our God when the time comes, but will help to build up his kingdom now?

As Latter-day Saints we must "have an eye single to the glory of God" and his work, not to our own ease and convenience. We must be enthusiastic builders in his kingdom, not just drifters on the sea of life.

The today for which we should live is embodied in the restored gospel of Jesus Christ. It is his day and ours.

IT IS VERILY TRUE

The entire restoration of the gospel consisted of a series of wondrous miracles. It had to be that way. How could the gospel be given from heaven to man otherwise?

Immortality *had* to communicate with mortality. And it did.

One of the very remarkable things about the restoration was the appearance of the angel Moroni to the Prophet Joseph Smith on September 21, 1823.

Angelic ministry was well known to the early Christians, but for centuries no such visitation had occurred, so far had the powers of godliness been lost to men.

But now a new day was dawning. The time had come for the fulfilment of prophecy. It had been divinely said that an angel would fly through the midst of heaven in the hour of God's judgment, returning the everlasting gospel to the earth to be preached to every nation, kindred, tongue and people.

The angel came. His appearance was in a small farm house in western New York. He was clothed in heavenly light. He spoke to a young man who had prayed for guidance. Three years earlier this youth had received a vision of our Heavenly Father and the Lord Jesus Christ. They gave him to understand that further light would be given him. And now it came.

Joseph Smith had been praying in his bedroom, prior to retiring for the night. He wrote:

"While I was thus in the act of calling upon God, I discovered a light appearing in my room, which continued to increase until the room was lighter than at noonday, when immediately a personage appeared at my bedside, standing in the air, for his feet did not touch the floor.

"He called me by name, and said unto me that he was a messenger sent from the presence of God to me, and that his name was Moroni; that God had a work for me to do." (Joseph Smith 2:30, 33.)

The visitor then told Joseph about the ancient record which he had completed after his father, Mormon, had compiled it. Now it was to be made public, and Joseph would be the instrument in the hands of God to do it.

That record was the Book of Mormon, which now is being carried to all parts of the free world as a testimony to the nations that God has spoken again from heaven, and now has restored his church and kingdom upon the earth preparatory to the second coming of the Savior.

Nearly four million living members of the Church declare that this is true. Other millions who, in the past, read and loved that book prior to their passing away, likewise testified to its truth.

Each anniversary is a reminder to Church members of this great fact, and it affords us all an opportunity to renew our efforts to spread its joyful message to our families, our neighbors and friends, and to the righteous everywhere.

The Book of Mormon is of divine origin. It was translated and published by the power of God. And it is true!

THE GOOD SHEPHERD

When Jesus came among men, most of them rejected him. Only a few became his true followers.

On the day of Pentecost, following the Crucifixion and Resurrection, only 120 came to the meeting of the saints. Where were the admiring throngs who cast their cloaks in his way during the triumphal entry into Jerusalem? Where were the thousands who sought the loaves and fishes? Where were the sick, the halt and the blind — now healed by his beneficence?

Reflected in their absence were his words from the Sermon on the Mount: "Strait is the gate, and narrow is the way, which leadeth unto life, and few there be that find it." (Matthew 7:14.)

Yet he was the Good Shepherd. He gave his life for the sheep. Not only did he go into the mountains seeking the lost one, but he gave his life for the entire flock, teaching that "it is not the will of your Father which is in heaven, that one of these little ones should perish." (Matthew 18:14.)

"I am the good shepherd. . . ." and "the good shepherd giveth his life for the sheep." (John 10:14, 11.)

The infinite love of the Shepherd for his flock cannot be measured by finite minds, for his was an infinite atonement.

Dare we turn our backs upon such a Shepherd?

There are those who claim he never lived. Others say he was not a shepherd at all, that he was but a transient rabbi, a good man to be sure, even a learned man (although there is no record that he ever went to school), but just a man.

Jesus was conscious of all this. His rejection by the populace was not easy for him. At the last, he sweat drops of blood in his anguish. But rejected or not, accepted by only a few, he nevertheless was the Good Shepherd. No adverse public opinion could change that. No rules or laws or philosophies or denunciations could alter this great fact.

He was led as a lamb to the slaughter — the Shepherd now a lamb, the sacrificial paschal Lamb — and crucified by those who said, "His blood be on us and on our children." A soul-chilling cry!

But whose is the ultimate victory? The crucifiers? Pilate's? Or Christ's? With what pity we now look back upon the blind and stubborn souls who scourged him and denounced him, and finally took his life!

Whose life did they really take? Was it their own eternal life?

Then whose souls were saved? The Marys, the Marthas, the Peters, the Jameses, the Johns, the Pauls, men like Barnabas, women like Dorcas?

Do we have them today? What modern souls will be saved? Are there those today who scourge Jesus in their minds, who reject him and his teachings even these many centuries after his ministry? Many do.

And what of those who lead the present-day sheep astray? Will the Good Shepherd, who still seeks to gather his flock, reward those who scatter them abroad? And with what reward?

He is the Good Shepherd. His flock is here today. Like Peter, we must feed his sheep and shelter his lambs, worldwide, that there may be one fold and one Shepherd.

OUR RAPID EXPANSION

The organization of new stakes in Hong Kong and Taiwan is further evidence of the rapid growth of the Church and its expansion into the far reaches of the earth.

For years the Saints in those two areas have looked forward to stakehood. They have carried on a splendid program in the missions, and have adopted the program of the Church even in the smallest branches.

What an inspiration it is to see oriental congregations meet in humble worship each Sabbath day! What a stimulating thing to hear them sing the songs of Zion in their native tongues!

We now have stakes in Japan, Korea, and the Philippines, as well as in Hong Kong and Taiwan, and as the work goes on, others will be formed.

The Church now has more than 750 stakes. Every state in the American union is covered by stakes now. There are twenty stakes in Great Britain, a similar number on continental Europe, one of the most recent having been organized in Paris, France.

Stakes now are to be found from South Africa to Sweden, from Hong Kong to Australia, from Denmark to the South Seas, and from South America to Alaska.

The Lord is hastening his work. The Church is advancing with great rapidity. A new day of expanded worldwide activity has dawned. It is thrilling to be a part of it.

THE WORLDWIDE CHURCH

All the world is our field, and all the men and women and boys and girls are potential servants of God.

When the Savior told his prophets to take the gospel into every nation, to every tongue and people, he opened a vista to them which was all-embracing. The gospel is for everyone. There are no privileged ones in the eyes of God. All who will come unto him may come.

But if they come they must take his yoke upon them, and that is a yoke of devotion to him and his high principles.

The gospel is now in about seventy nations. The priesthood functions there, and the Saints gather together in humility to worship the Lord. They give thanks for his mercy in restoring the gospel in these latter days; they teach their children the faith. A people is being made ready to greet the Master when he comes!

The conferences in South America are but further evidence of this great movement, and they too will have far-reaching effects. Similar conferences held in Europe, Mexico, the Orient, and the South Pacific have been a great blessing to the people living in those lands. A renewed spirit of enthusiasm, devotion, and brotherly love marked the Saints during those inspiring meetings, and it still persists. The work goes on at an accelerated rate.

One of the great blessings of these area conferences is that they bring to the people in distant lands the opportunity to see and hear the prophet, seer and revelator of the Church. Most of the Saints living so far away have never attended a general conference in Salt Lake City. Most of them never will. So, in their inspired manner, the presidents of the Church have taken the conferences to the people. President Joseph Fielding Smith, President Harold B. Lee, and President Spencer W. Kimball were shown these new horizons to the Lord's work, and promptly responded.

They have humbly but devotedly extended every effort to fulfill this new purpose which projects the inspiration of the gospel to distant fields.

General conferences in Salt Lake City are broadcast to many nations of the world, and the Saints flock to hear the Brethren speak. But an area conference is different in that the people can feel the living presence of the Lord's prophets.

They can see as well as hear, and with greater knowledge and appreciation they return to their homes with more determination than ever to serve the Lord and keep his commandments.

The work of the Church goes on. It will continue to grow and flourish, despite the problems which assail so many nations economically and politically. Eventually the gospel will fill the earth in preparation for the glorious millennial reign of our Lord and Savior, Jesus Christ.

WHAT JULY TWENTY-FOURTH MEANS

What does Pioneer Day mean to us who live today? To the pioneers themselves it meant the end of a long and arduous journey. It also meant the end of one chapter in Church history, and the opening of another.

It meant, too, the fulfillment of a great prophecy in which Isaiah declared that the work of the Lord would be carried to the tops of the mountains, that a temple would be built there, and that people from all nations would come to it. They would come seeking for a knowledge of the word of God, that they might truly learn of him and then walk in his paths.

To the pioneers it was a significant day indeed, but what does it mean to us? Of course, we all honor those hardy emigrants who left their all in the East to make their homes in the Great Basin. But do we honor them merely because they were so hardy, so skillful in making the desert blossom as the rose? That is the tendency among many.

We of today should go far beyond that. We shall be recreant indeed if we do not remember the purpose of their coming to Utah and if we fail to recognize the divine hand which directed them.

They came here to fulfill prophecy. They came here because God gave them the restored gospel and made them the custodians of the modern kingdom of God on earth. They were divinely chosen to perform the work, difficult as was their assignment.

They came here to establish that kingdom firmly upon the rock which would never fail, that from this rock the good word of God may go to the nations as it now is going.

They came here to raise families in the faith, to rear sons and daughters so full of conviction, so dedicated, so willing to sacrifice that they would even give their lives if necessary to take the restored gospel abroad, and some have made this sacrifice.

"Seek ye first the kingdom of heaven" was the watchword. Testimony was their moving power.

The generation still being reared now holds the torch handed to them by our noble pioneers, and together with an army of new converts, they take the word to every open door.

We are, of necessity, a proselyting Church. We are commanded of God to take the word throughout the world. Is there any better way of observing Pioneer Day than for us who live today to dedicate ourselves to the same great cause that motivated them?

Can we do better than to build on their foundations and do so with the same kind of resolute purpose?

We, too, are pioneers in God's great latter-day work and must continue to be so until every corner of the earth has been reached with his divine message.

WHEN WE SAY "AMEN"

It has been a custom in the Church from the time of its organization for members to repeat an "amen" after prayers and sermons, but it is not alone a custom in our church. Nor is it something that originated with the Latter-day Saints. Many Christians follow this custom, although it has nearly disappeared from many congregations.

The use of "amen" is biblical in its origin. "Amen" was used by commandment of the Lord in ancient times, and it had a particular meaning. Some have supposed that it was merely an expression of assent on the part of an audience, but it was much more meaningful than that.

Although one definition suggests the assent, "so be it," the larger sense given to this expression is more like the binding of a covenant.

The Bible dictionary says: "Amen, literally, true, and used as a substantive, 'that which is true,' fixing as it were the stamp of truth upon the assertion which is accompanied, *and making it binding as an oath.*"

Anciently in both synagogues and private houses it was customary for the people or members of the family who were present to say "amen" after the prayers which were offered.

The Savior taught it, and closed the Lord's Prayer with an amen. (Matthew 6:13.) Paul taught it to the Corinthians. (1 Corinthians 14:16.)

David ended Psalm 106 with the words: "Blessed be the Lord God of Israel from everlasting to everlasting: and let all the people say, Amen. Praise ye the Lord."

When the Lord gave instructions against the use of images in worship, he spoke through Moses and said: "Cursed be the man that makes any graven or molten images; an abomination unto the Lord, the work of the craftsman, and putteth it in a secret place. And all the people shall answer and say Amen." The commandment to say amen — binding the people as an agreement — was required of them by revelation.

In modern times the Lord put a similar interpretation on the word as he said: "And he that cometh in and is faithful before me, and is a brother, or if they be brethren, they shall salute the president or teacher with uplifted hands to heaven, with the same prayer and covenant, or by saying Amen, in token of the same." (D&C 88:135.)

In the only prayers the Lord has given by revelation for our continued use — the baptismal prayer and those on the sacrament — he himself used the expression *Amen.*

The dedicatory prayer for the Kirtland Temple was given by revelation to the Prophet Joseph. It ended with "Amen and Amen."

Anciently the word of the Lord was: "And all the people shall answer and say Amen."

The presiding brethren of today ask our congregations now to answer also with the expression *Amen* — following sermons and prayers.

It is a custom to be preserved in the Church. It is one in which all should join. In a very real sense it is an expression of rededication and acceptance, a pledge of obedience.

THE LINES ARE DRAWN

The lines between the forces of God and the forces of the adversary are being drawn more tightly each day.

It is not that the rules of God's kingdom have varied; it is that the intrusions and infiltrations of the wicked one are increasing by leaps and bounds. No doubt he realizes that his time is getting short.

But the lines are there, clear and sharp. It is for every faithful follower of Christ to recognize this fact, and to build stronger bulwarks day by day to resist the "fiery darts of the adversary" as the apostle Paul expressed it.

More than ever, a wholehearted acceptance of the existence of God becomes a necessity. The adversary would make atheists of us all, if he could, or would lead us into the worship of false gods, which suits his purpose quite as well.

Acceptance of Jesus as the Christ becomes equally vital to our welfare. Again the adversary tempts us to deny him, seeking to enslave us in doing so.

Acceptance of the rules of clean living, virtue, chastity, sobriety, integrity, honesty — and righteousness in general — is the only path to safety. Wickedness never was happiness. Only in Christ may the abundant life be found.

Recognition of the fact that Satan is a reality — an enemy to our welfare — is likewise imperative for each one of us, for that demon has declared war upon the Saints "and encompasseth them round about."

Who's on the Lord's side? Now is the time to show!

2.

PROPHETS AND REVELATION

DEAD MEN TELL TALES

A headline on a newspaper article read: "Dead Men Tell Many Tales." The article referred to the commentary of a British scientist with respect to the discovery of some prehistoric bones.

The scholar said that from even small bits of bones found in remote places, "paleopathologists can build up a picture of what people were like [prehistoric ones that is], what they ate, the clothes they wore, how they treated their teeth [some people used them as tools], the weapons they used and the medicine they practiced."

All of which shows that one portion of bone plus a greater portion of imagination becomes the basis for many peculiar theories that even find their way into our school textbooks.

But dead men do tell tales — tales of truth and veracity, tales of faith and salvation — if the right "dead" men speak. To this the Latter-day Saints can testify.

This Church in large measure is based upon men coming back from the dead and bringing light and truth as part of the restoration of the gospel.

Moroni, who lived about 400 A.D., came back in full physical form, and delivered to Joseph Smith the Book of Mormon.

John the Baptist, once beheaded by Herod, came back and ordained Joseph and Oliver Cowdery to the Aaronic Priesthood.

Peter, James and John, the ancient apostles of nearly two thousand years ago, came to Joseph and Oliver and gave to them the holy Melchizedek Priesthood and the apostleship.

The prophet Elijah, who lived about 850 B.C., visited Joseph and Oliver in the Kirtland Temple, as did Elias, who lived in the days of ancient Father Abraham.

Adam came and Noah came, as did "diverse other angels," each one delivering the powers of his office to be used in this dispensation of the fulness of times.

These men who once lived on the earth, but who now came back in full reality, told many "tales," testimonies of truth regarding their work and the perpetuity of the gospel, conferring their sacred powers on modern men.

And they didn't base their conclusions upon bone fragments and scholastic imagination either.

THE BASIC PRINCIPLE

When the Prophet Joseph Smith was asked to define the difference between The Church of Jesus Christ of Latter-day Saints and other Christian denominations, his brief reply was: "We have the Holy Ghost."

It was a significant remark, and is basic to the entire concept of Mormonism.

What does it mean to "have the Holy Ghost"? And what are the characteristics of this divine gift that its possession defines the difference between our church and all others?

The Holy Ghost is essentially a revelator. The Savior made it clear that the Holy Ghost will take of the things of the Father and "show them unto you." He will "teach you all things" and will "guide you into all truth." He will even "show you things to come." (John 15, 16.)

People who possess the Holy Ghost, then, may receive revelation from heaven for their own particular needs. In addition, there are living prophets of the Church who are given the word of God by revelation for the instruction of the entire membership.

They are placed in the Church "for the perfecting of the saints, for the work of the ministry, for the edifying of the body of Christ." (Ephesians 4:12.)

Prophecy and current revelation, then, characterize the church which has the Holy Ghost. This explains why the Prophet Joseph made this distinction. He himself was a prophet and understood prophecy. He received revelation. His close associates likewise were prophets, seers and revelators.

This fact drew the line between these men and adherents of all other faiths. And it still does, for what other church believes in modern prophecy?

In our Church today we have living prophets, seers, and revelators constantly functioning in their divine responsibility for the perfecting of the Saints, for the work of the ministry and for the edifying of the body of Christ.

It is most significant that the Lord spoke of these men as follows:

"They shall speak as they are moved upon by the Holy Ghost.

"And whatsoever they shall speak when moved upon by the Holy Ghost shall be scripture, shall be the will of the Lord, shall be the mind of the Lord, shall be the word of the Lord, shall be the voice of the Lord, and the power of God unto salvation." (D&C 68:3, 4.)

This is a fundamental principle which continues within the Church. It was not confined to Joseph Smith's day, nor to the time of Brigham Young. It continues in and with the Church, for the Church must move by current revelations, otherwise there would be confusion.

Our prophets of today speak from the Tabernacle in general conference. Particularly as our President speaks, let us remember that his message will be that of the mouthpiece of God — the prophet, seer and revelator for today!

Important developments are rapidly occurring in both the Church and the world, and every one of us will be affected by what the future unfolds.

How thankful we should be for the great principle of our religion which says: "We believe all that God has revealed, all that He does now reveal, and we believe that He will yet reveal many great and important things pertaining to the kingdom of God." (Ninth Article of Faith.)

And how grateful we should be that we have living prophets through whom this knowledge will come!

We are blessed people. With confidence we may face an uncertain future, having inspired men "to guide us in these latter days."

STAND BY YOUR CHIEF

Long before President David O. McKay became the leader of the Church, he issued a clarion call to the general membership appealing to them to stand by and sustain their prophet, seer and revelator.

Said he in October of 1934: "I uphold before you this morning the President of this church as God's representative, divinely appointed, and say to all Israel: *Stand by your chief!*

"Let that spirit of unity and oneness for which our Lord and Savior prayed on the night of his betrayal be characteristic of this, his Church: Father keep them one, as Thou and I are one."

The Saints have been divinely promised that if they will follow the President of the Church, they will never go astray, because the Lord will not allow his prophet, seer and revelator to lead them from the proper path of their duty.

This has been demonstrated frequently in the past. President Joseph F. Smith discoursed emphatically upon this subject, and pointed to each of his own predecessors as men without guile, who were led by the Spirit of God in their administrations.

He spoke of the testimony of Joseph Smith, whose blood was shed in martyrdom, and declared: "His testimony is now and has been in force among the children of men as verily as the blood of Jesus Christ is in force. It is a binding testimony upon all the world. It has been from the day his blood was shed until now and will continue until the winding-up scene."

He bore testimony to the leadership of Brigham Young in bringing the Saints to the Rockies, "which was done by the will of heaven and by the guiding power of the Holy Ghost." President Young was God's mouthpiece for that day, and the people who followed him prospered, whereas the splinter groups which drifted away never did.

He spoke, too, of John Taylor, "a man honest to the core," who was "guided by inspiration in the performance of his duty, far more than by any gift of wisdom or of judgment that he himself possessed."

He spoke likewise of Wilford Woodruff, "a man without guile" who led the people through one of their most serious crises, and again, those who followed the President prospered, while those who refused came to naught.

Of Lorenzo Snow he spoke similarly. In discussing each of his predecessors, he demonstrated that the Spirit of God guided them, and that in crisis after crisis which came to the Church, those who followed the President were blessed and prospered while those who did not eventually fell away.

It is the same today. Our present First Presidency is inspired as were all of their predecessors. They continue to lead the Church by the direction of the Holy Spirit. But it is not alone the men we follow — it is the Almighty God who directs them. We therefore follow both God and his prophets as we accept his word through them.

This great lesson was taught by the Lord himself on the day when the Church was organized. He said to the membership concerning the President:

"Wherefore, meaning the church, thou shalt give heed unto all his words and commandments which he shall give unto you as he receiveth them, walking in all holiness before me;

"For his word ye shall receive, as if from mine own mouth, in all patience and faith."

And if we do, what is the promise?

"By doing these things the gates of hell shall not prevail against you; yea, and the Lord God will disperse the powers of darkness from before you, and cause the heavens to shake for your good and his name's glory." (D&C 21:4-6.)

Is there anything we need in this troubled world quite as much as a fulfilment of that promise? And how may we receive it? There is but one way: "His word ye shall receive, as if from mine own mouth, in all patience and faith."

Then what shall we do? Accept the advice of President McKay and follow our leader for today: *"Stand by your chief!"*

PRESIDENT'S AUTHORITY

The President of the Church today holds all of the keys, priesthood and powers that were given by the angels to the Prophet Joseph Smith for the restoration of the gospel. Before the Prophet Joseph was martyred, he conferred upon all members of the Council of Twelve Apostles the keys and authorities which he had received from the ministering angels.

Some of these powers are referred to in the Doctrine and Covenants, section 110, and others also are spoken of in section

128. It is well known that the Aaronic Priesthood, restored by John the Baptist, and the Melchizedek Priesthood and the apostleship, as restored by Peter, James and John, were given to the Prophet early in his ministry.

Joseph knew that the Twelve were to carry the restored gospel to all nations, and must therefore continually hold and be empowered to exercise the keys of the priesthood, which would continue in the Church even after his death, a thing he well understood. Otherwise, how could the work go on?

As early as February 27, 1835, according to minutes kept by Oliver Cowdery, in answer to a question pertaining to the Twelve the Prophet Joseph Smith said: "They are to hold the keys of this ministry, to unlock the door of the Kingdom of heaven unto all nations, and to preach the Gospel to every creature." (DHC 2:200.)

On March 27, 1836, the Prophet recorded in his own documentary history that in the Kirtland Temple he had called upon the Saints to sustain the Twelve Apostles as prophets, seers, revelators and special witnesses "to all the nations of the earth, holding the keys of the kingdom." (DHC 2:417.)

On August 16, 1841, the Prophet addressed the Saints and said that the time had come when the Twelve should be called upon to stand in their place next to the First Presidency "to bear off the kingdom victoriously to the nations." (DHC 4:403.)

The Prophet conferred all of these keys upon the Twelve, as is testified to by various of the early Brethren. Heber C. Kimball quoted the Prophet as saying, "I have conferred upon them all the power, priesthood, and authority that God ever conferred upon me." (JD 1:206.)

President Wilford Woodruff quoted the Prophet as saying at another time while addressing the Twelve: "Now I have received as prophet, seer and revelator, standing at the head of this dispensation, every key, every ordinance, every principle, and every priesthood that belongs to the last dispensation and fulness of times, and I have sealed all these things upon your heads." (CR, April 1898, p. 89.)

Orson Hyde testified similarly. President Brigham Young said: "Joseph conferred upon our heads all the keys and powers belonging to the apostleship which he himself held before he was taken away." (DHC 7:230.)

Each new apostle ordained in the Church today receives these same powers, and when any apostle becomes the senior member and President of the Church, he not only holds all of these keys but is authorized to use them.

FOLLOW THE PRESIDENT

When the late President Joseph Fielding Smith addressed a general conference, he made a significant statement pertaining to the presidency of the Church.

Said he: "I testify that if we shall look to the First Presidency and follow their counsel and direction, no power on earth can stay or change our course as a church, and as individuals we shall gain peace in this life and be inheritors of eternal glory in the world to come. And I say this to you, my good brethren, in the name of the Lord Jesus Christ."

Other presidents before him also have said that if we follow the leadership of the First Presidency we shall never go astray nor apostatize from the truth.

The Lord himself made a stirring declaration regarding this point. On the day the Church was organized, the Lord formally made the President of the Church the prophet, seer and revelator, and then said this to the membership pertaining to the President:

"Wherefore, meaning the church, thou shalt give heed unto all his words and commandments which he shall give unto you as he receiveth them, walking in all holiness before me;

"For his word ye shall receive, as if from mine own mouth, in all patience and faith.

"For by doing these things the gates of hell shall not prevail against you; yea, and the Lord God will disperse the powers of darkness from before you, and cause the heavens to shake for your good and his name's glory." (D&C 21:4-6.)

THE MEN WHO GUIDE US

It was no idle expression when Amos of old said: "Surely the Lord God will do nothing, but he revealeth his secret unto his servants the prophets." (Amos 3:7.)

Nor was it any attempt at mere rhetoric when Paul wrote that the inspired leaders of the church are given of the Lord "for the perfecting of the saints, for the work of the ministry, for the edifying of the body of Christ." (Ephesians 4:12.)

Neither was it a mere passing remark when he said that these leaders are given us "that we henceforth be no more children, tossed to and fro, and carried about with every wind of doctrine." (Ephesians 4:14.)

Throughout the centuries there have been true prophets and false prophets, just as there have been varying and conflicting creeds and churches.

When the Savior told the Nephites the name by which his church should be called, he gave us an important key. If it was called after a man, it was the church of a man; if it was called after Christ, then it was Christ's church. *If.*

And that *if* gives us the answer regarding both churches and preachers: *"If* it so be that they are built upon my gospel." (3 Nephi 27:8.)

The prophets of The Church of Jesus Christ of Latter-day Saints are indeed "built upon my gospel," and so is the Church which they represent. And so are the teachings which they give to us at the general conferences and otherwise as their ministry blesses us.

They show us the way of truth — the way to salvation. They speak for the Lord, and in his name, and when he gives this inspired guidance, "whether by mine own voice or by the voice of my servants, it is the same." (D&C 1:38.)

That is why he spoke later about the same matter and said: "Whatsoever they shall speak when moved upon by the Holy Ghost shall be scripture, shall be the will of the Lord, shall be the mind of the Lord, shall be the word of the Lord, shall be the voice of the Lord, and the power of God unto salvation." (D&C 68:4.)

We indeed need divine guidance, for we are living in troublous times. We are attacked by confusion, by false teachings, theories and hypotheses, by seduction and all other forms of vice.

Have we the strength to stand?

Have we the wisdom to sort out good from evil?

Have we the faith to accept the divine teachings despite the persuasive theories of men?

If we believe in God, we must realize that our salvation rests upon our decision to "seek first the kingdom of God and his righteousness." Conflicting theories, or assaults upon our morals, or the lure of fame and fortune should not be allowed to interfere.

God does live. He does have his inspired spokesmen on earth once again. Our attitude toward them may determine our eternal destiny.

Though these men be humble; though they may have few worldly honors; though they may even seem commonplace to us, the fact remains that they are the prophets of God, and that they speak for him.

We cannot hope for salvation if we go contrary to the divine word.

THE SPIRIT OF PROPHECY

The General Authorities of the Church may be everyday acquaintances to many, particularly their old friends from school, business, ward or stake; but let us remember that they are also the spokesmen for God in these present days.

They are a humble group. They have no selfish desires, no urge for personal aggrandizement. They have broken hearts and contrite spirits and have an eye single to the glory of God, as the scriptures say. But when they speak by the power of the Lord, let us remember that they give us the divine will. (D&C 68.)

Too many people believe the dead prophets, but feel perfectly justified in turning their backs upon and even criticizing the living ones.

We sustain the First Presidency and the Twelve particularly as prophets, seers and revelators. This is no idle gesture. It is significant, and has deep and profound meaning. It has a vital bearing upon our eternal salvation.

One of the earliest lessons the Lord taught, even before the organization of the Church, was: "Deny not the spirit of revelation, nor the spirit of prophecy, for wo unto him that denieth these things." (D&C 11:25.)

This should be ever in our minds when we think of the men who give us divine direction. Let us not regard these brethren merely as old friends who have "climbed high in the Church." God has called them out from among us, and has made them his spokesmen to guide us in these latter days.

THE LORD'S WARNING

It was so in the past; it is so now. Some men and women still rise up claiming new revelations for the Church, and there always seem to be some who believe them.

But why need anyone be deceived by such false teachers? The Lord is not inconsistent. He does not establish competitive systems within his kingdom. He has but one voice to the Church and that is the voice of its president, duly appointed as prophet, seer and revelator.

At the very inception of our latter-day work, impostors arose claiming new revelations for the Church, but which were contrary to the already revealed word and will of God.

Some of these people used "peep stones"; some buried their faces in a hat; others held hands in an occult circle; some used various other devices, or none at all (merely saying that they heard celestial voices), but all claimed supernatural gifts. In some cases their performances were simply hoaxes perpetrated upon the public. Others undoubtedly did have supernatural experiences, but not from the Lord.

There are still some arising and making deceptive claims, some with regard to "dream mines," some pertaining to other types of business, or to plural marriage, and some making false claims to divine authority. But the Lord has spoken plainly about them, and what he said is published in our modern scripture so that all may read and know and understand and, as the Lord himself said, none shall be deceived. But in spite of all that, gullible ones still believe these false claims and are led astray by them. The tragedy of it is that in their deception they also lose their souls' salvation.

To make his word clear and to give all fair warning against false prophets, the Lord said:

"For behold, verily, verily, I say unto you, that ye have received a commandment for a law unto my church, through him whom I have appointed unto you to receive commandments and revelations from my hand.

"And this ye shall know assuredly — that there is none other appointed unto you to receive commandments and revelations until he be taken, if he abide in me.

"But verily, verily, I say unto you, that none else shall be appointed unto this gift except it be through him; for if it be taken from him he shall not have power except to appoint another in his stead.

"And this shall be a law unto you, *that ye receive not the teachings of any that shall come before you as revelations or commandments;*

"*And this I give unto you that you may not be deceived, that you may know they are not of me.*

"For verily I say unto you, that he that is ordained of me shall come in at the gate and be ordained as I have told you before, to teach those revelations which you have received and shall receive through him whom I have appointed." (D&C 43:2-7. Italics added.) (See also D&C 20:65; 28:11-13.)

The false prophets are not ordained of God, they are not appointed by the President of the Church as the scripture prescribes, and they are not sustained by the vote of the people as the Lord requires. Obviously, then, they are not of God. With warnings and safeguards such as the Lord provides, need anyone be deceived? If we follow the President of the Church, we need never go astray.

YES, WE BELIEVE

The burden of the Savior's message was that we should believe and not doubt his divine teachings. This was stressed to doubting Thomas following the Resurrection. It formed the theme of his miracles, as he said: "Thy faith hath made thee whole."

He pleaded with the people to believe him, as the Son of God, and to accept his truths. Faith, he knew, was the moving power which all required for salvation.

It is written so in our Articles of Faith. They begin with "we believe" in every paragraph but one, and that one says that we claim the right to believe and worship as we wish.

One of these articles reads: "We believe all that God has revealed, all that He does now reveal, and we believe that He will yet reveal many great and important things pertaining to the Kingdom of God."

In other words, we not only accept the divine revelations of the past, but we believe in and expect divine guidance for the here and now, and likewise for the future.

It is by sacred determination that we have prophets, seers and revelators in the Church. They speak by the power of the Holy Ghost, and "whatsoever they shall speak when moved upon by the Holy Ghost shall be scripture, shall be the will of the Lord, shall be the mind of the Lord, shall be the word of the Lord, shall be the voice of the Lord, and the power of God unto salvation." (D&C 68:4.)

We hear these prophets at our general conferences. Some people complain that they do not say with each word, "thus saith the Lord," but is that necessary since they nevertheless speak by the power of God?

Said President Wilford Woodruff: "Read the life of Brigham Young and you can hardly find a revelation wherein he said 'thus saith the Lord'; but the Holy Ghost was with him; he taught by inspiration and revelation. . . .

"Joseph said, 'thus saith the Lord' almost every day of his life in laying the foundation of this work. But those who followed him have not deemed it always necessary to say 'thus saith the Lord'; yet they have led the people by the power of the Holy Ghost." (*Deseret News,* November 7, 1891.)

President Woodruff then continued: "I do not want the Latter-day Saints to understand that the Lord is not with us and that he is not giving revelations to us; for he is giving us revelation and will give us revelation until this scene is wound up."

It is so today. We have now, as formerly, prophets, seers and revelators at the head of the Church. As formerly, also, they do receive divine guidance, and speak in very deed as the prophets of God, as the voice of God, and they hold the power of God unto salvation.

It is for the Saints to accept this principle, as their own Articles of Faith declare, and be believing, and not be as Thomas, allowing themselves to doubt our inspired leaders. Without faith is it impossible to please God.

THE RIGHT TO SPEAK

Who has the right to speak for God? There are many who assume to do so, as there always have been. But who really may speak for the Almighty?

When Jesus began his ministry, people were astonished by his teachings, because he spoke as one having authority.

When Paul and Peter, James and John, and others of their day, addressed themselves to the public, they also spoke as having authority; and this for one reason: they actually did have the authority. The mantle of power was upon them. The Holy Ghost inspired them. They received revelation, and it was revelation which they uttered. Hence they spoke for God.

It has been so from the beginning. Do we recall the words of Amos? "Surely the Lord God will do nothing, but he revealeth his secret to his servants the prophets." (Amos 3:7.)

That was God's plan. He spoke through his prophets. They were the ones authorized to speak for him.

In Jesus' day there were many who pretended to speak for God, but without either authority or revelation. They manufactured their own creeds, but these the Savior rejected, saying that even their worship was in vain, since they taught for doctrine the commandments of men. (Matthew 15:9.)

He referred to false teachers also in his Sermon on the Mount. In the seventh chapter of Matthew we read:

"Many will say to me in that day, Lord, Lord, have we not prophesied in thy name? and in thy name have cast out devils? and in thy name done many wonderful works?

"And then I will profess unto them, I never knew you: depart from me, ye that work iniquity." (Matthew 7:22-23.)

They spoke in his name, they prophesied in his name, and they performed miracles in his name; and yet he never knew them, and ordered them to depart, for they worked iniquity. Why? They were not his servants. And why? Because he had never authorized them, nor did he inspire them or give them revelations which would make it possible for them to speak for God.

The Authentic New Testament by Schonfield makes this passage clear: "Many will say to me at that time: Master, Master, have we not prophesied in thy name and in thy name performed many miracles?

"But then I shall tell them plainly, I have never authorized you. Be off with you, you illegal practitioners."

But today authorized prophets speak again. Once more we have the ministrations of apostles and prophets; once more we have revelation; once again the Holy Ghost moves upon the Lord's chosen servants. Those prophets speak as they have done in the past. And what has the Lord said about the utterances of his chosen servants?

He said this, plainly and specifically:

"They shall speak as they are moved upon by the Holy Ghost.

"And whatsoever they shall speak when moved upon by the Holy Ghost shall be scripture, shall be the will of the Lord, shall be the mind of the Lord, shall be the word of the Lord, shall be the voice of the Lord, and the power of God unto salvation." (D&C 68:3, 4.)

When he spoke to the members of the Church about the President of the Church, God said:

"Thou shalt give heed unto all his words and commandments which he shall give unto you as he receiveth them, walking in all holiness before me;

"For his word ye shall receive, as if from mine own mouth, in all patience and faith."

And he promised this to his Saints if they would obey:

"For by doing these things the gates of hell shall not prevail against you; yea, and the Lord God will disperse the powers of darkness from before you, and cause the heavens to shake for your good, and his name's glory." (D&C 21:4-6.)

So at conference time, when we hear the words of the prophets, we have opportunity to pledge allegiance to the Lord and his latter-day work.

PROPHECY FULFILLED

We often speak of prophecies concerning the latter days, and their fulfillment. Some are being fulfilled at this present time. One of the most remarkable instances is the unfolding of Book of Mormon predictions concerning the Lamanites and their emergence as recipients of God's great blessings in latter days. Many are the scriptural references to their development, and remarkable is the fulfillment that is now taking place.

The scriptures spoke of the manner in which the Lamanites would first be driven and scattered, but that afterward they would begin to believe in Christ and be numbered with his church. Note just a few facts concerning them as presented in the December 1975 *Ensign* magazine:

There are thirty stakes in the Church with predominantly Lamanite membership.

It is estimated that there are three hundred fifty thousand members of the Church who are of Lamanite descent. This is about 10 percent of the total membership.

The Church has established excellent schools for people of Lamanite blood in the Pacific islands, in Mexico, Central America, and South America. Some sixteen thousand students are enrolled in them, mostly of Lamanite descent.

Another thirteen thousand are enrolled in seminary classes near public and federal schools in the United States and Canada.

A kindergarten seminary system serves still another 12,500 from forty tribes in twenty states of the American Union and five Canadian provinces.

Fifteen hundred attend Brigham Young University at its Provo and Hawaiian campuses.

Lamanite students have earned 260 baccalaureate and advanced degrees from BYU in fifty-four different fields of study.

A remarkable development has been the effort of the Church to teach illiterate Indians, particularly of South America, to read and write.

Reading is taught phonetically, and one thousand such Indians have learned to read, thus opening a whole new life to them.

The Book of Mormon prophecies are being fulfilled among those peoples. Advancement will continue. The day of the Lamanite has dawned, and they are responding to the opportunities given them.

HEAR YE HIM!

What are the three most significant statements in all holy writ?

Without a doubt, one of them must be: "Unto you is born this day in the city of David a Saviour, which is Christ the Lord." (Luke 2:11.) All creation waited for that joyous event.

And what is a second? Could it be other than: "He is risen," the thrilling words of the angel announcing the resurrection of the Lord?

And what should be the third? Our Heavenly Father expressed it on several occasions. At the time of the Transfiguration his words were heard in this vital instruction: "Hear ye him."

When the Father addressed the boy prophet Joseph Smith, introducing Jesus the Christ to the young man, he again used those same words: "Hear ye him."

How often these words are referred to! Generally they are spoken of as a part of a narration of the great events leading up to these expressions. But do we regard them as commands?

Commands they are, from the Almighty himself. Commands they are to us who are believers in the Christ. They command us to hear the Savior, to hearken to what he says, and to obey.

The scripture often speaks of people who have ears but hear not. Shall we be included in that grouping? We of today have ears, and they are given to us that we may hear — hear the words and instruction of the Savior of the world. That we may do this, the Lord commands us to search the scriptures, which will guide us toward eternal life.

But he does more than that. He provides prophets through whom he speaks — living prophets — men we can see and hear and know, men who speak the words of God under the inspiration of the Holy Ghost.

And when they thus speak, what does the Lord say? "Whether by mine own voice or by the voice of my servants, it is the same." (D&C 1:38.) But then he adds this concerning his prophets who live among the Saints of latter days: "Whatsoever they shall speak when moved upon by the Holy Ghost shall be scripture, shall be the will of the Lord, shall be the mind of the Lord, shall be the voice of the Lord, and the power of God unto salvation." (D&C 68:4.)

During general conferences we hear the word of the Lord as spoken by his representatives here on earth. It is a great opportunity, for these are the men whose words, under the inspiration of the Holy Ghost, are to us the word and will of God.

The Eternal Father, speaking of the Christ, says: "Hear ye him." It is a significant commandment. That same Christ commands that we hearken to his word as it is given us by his chosen servants, "and whatsoever they shall speak when moved upon by the Holy Ghost shall be scripture."

It is something to ponder, seriously.

If we have ears that will not hear, of course we will not hearken. And if we do not hearken to those words, can we hope for a blessing?

LIFE AND RESURRECTION

One of the greatest truths ever uttered is this: "I am the resurrection, and the life."

And Martha, who heard it, said to him who had thus spoken: "Thou art the Christ, the Son of God, which should come into the world." (John 11:25, 27.)

There were doubters in those days as there are doubters today, but the fact still remains: Christ is the resurrection and the life. He restored life, even as in the first place he gave it, for he is the Creator, the Redeemer, the Savior and the Messiah.

Who can look upon the death of a loved one and fail to feel a sense of immortality? Who can truly think that there is no hereafter?

Dr. Arthur Compton, world-renowned scientist and Nobel prize winner, writing for the *Los Angeles Times*, said:

"If we were to use our own best judgment, what would we say is the most important thing about a noble man? Would we not place first the beauty of his character? It takes a whole lifetime to build the character of a noble man.

"Having been thus perfected, what shall nature do with him? Annihilate him? What infinite waste!

"I prefer to believe that he lives on after death, continuing in a larger sphere, in cooperation with his Maker, the work he has here begun."

And so it is with nearly every one.

But who provides that immortality of which even the scientists speak? Certainly not the scientists, and not the politicians nor the educators nor the businessmen. They are all shocked and appalled at death. They stand before it helplessly. May most of them allow a spark of hope, if not of faith, to rise in their hearts and persuade them to believe in God!

Birth is unexplainable without God. So is death. And certainly is this true of immortality!

But to bring the dead back to life — only an infinite power can do that. And an infinite power did — the Divine Christ, who had within himself control of life and death and the ability to live again.

Jesus is the life of all. It is his Spirit which gives life and light to every creature. As he survived the grave, so shall we. As he lives now in his heavenly glory, so may we if we will but follow him.

Resurrection will come to all — good and evil, believers and unbelievers. But there are grades of resurrection, as Paul told the Corinthians. (1 Corinthians 15.) To receive the highest we must follow Christ in devoted obedience. That alone will qualify us for such a blessing.

Christ lives. As he came back from the grave, so shall we, but it will be only by his power, for he alone is the resurrection and the life.

IMMORTALITY IS REAL

To most people, birth and death are our two greatest mysteries. How many know from whence we came? How many know that birth is not the beginning of our existence?

And how many know what comes after death — whether there is life, or annihilation, or whether we just go to sleep, never to wake again?

The Latter-day Saints know the answers to those questions, and as a result find real meaning both in life and in death.

It is most reassuring to know that, as Paul said, "we are the offspring of God," that we are literally his spirit children, and that we are here in earthlife as a step in our eternal progression.

How enlightening to learn that we once lived with God, even before this earth was created, and that in fact the earth was made especially for us as our mortal home.

And how comforting it is to know that as our loved ones — or as we ourselves — pass from here that an endless life awaits us, as real and as exciting as this one ever could be.

And how grateful we should be to the Savior of mankind that he brought it all about. It was he who created the earth in the first place, that we, the children of the Eternal Father, might live here. It was he who overcame death, and gave us everlasting life. It was he who paid the penalty for sin, that all who repent and accept his gospel may partake of his redemption.

In giving us immortality, Jesus fulfilled the words of John, who said: "And God shall wipe away all tears from their eyes; and there shall be no more death, neither sorrow, nor crying, neither shall there be any more pain." (Revelation 21:4.)

Let us accept the testimonies of the prophets and the scriptures that life is everlasting, that the grave is not our goal, that as God lives eternally, so shall we, and that through his beneficent provision, loved ones shall meet again, and families may go on in happiness together forever and forever.

3.

DILIGENCE
AND
DEVOTION

HE EXPECTS DEVOTION

How much does the Lord expect of us in terms of devotion and obedience to his laws? Is it true that we may wilfully sin a little and then obey a little, hoping to receive but a few stripes and yet be saved?

How completely many people misunderstand their own religion, feeling that adherence to a few rituals takes care of the need.

We are not in the Church to "just get by" with the Lord. We are not engaged in some game of chance, depending alone on the infinite mercy of God. Nor are we in a situation of giving lip service to the various laws of the gospel.

In our religion we are in the business of building character, a thing which can never be achieved through lip service. The kind of character we are expected to build is one like Christ's. He meant every word when he taught: "Be ye therefore perfect, even as your Father which is in heaven is perfect." (Matthew 5:48.)

Ponder over those words — be perfect like your Heavenly Father!

There is no slothfulness.

There is no halfhearted service, no begrudging obedience, no mere show of piety, no hypocrisy.

There is no dishonesty, there is no filthy talk, there is no loosening of the moral code.

But there is love unfeigned. There is virtue, patience, long-suffering, kindness and charity. There is much of the Golden Rule, much of loving our neighbors as ourselves, and there is untiring devotion to divine principles.

If we want to know how perfect we must become, let us read Paul's definition in the fourth chapter of Ephesians. We must achieve unto the fullness of the measure of the stature of Christ!

That is what the Lord expects of his people. That is why he tells us that we must serve him with all our heart, might, mind and strength. (D&C 4:2.)

Can we hope to become Christlike with any less effort?

THAT CLEAR SIGNAL

A clear and certain signal was given to the Latter-day Saints in a recent general conference of the Church.

It was announced, echoed and re-echoed in general sessions, in auxiliary sessions, and in a seminar for Regional Representatives of the Twelve.

President Spencer W. Kimball and other General Authorities urged all officers to extend that clear signal throughout the Church and waken the membership to its full significance, arousing them to *action*.

In the days of the apostle Paul he complained to the Corinthians that if their "trumpet give an uncertain sound, who shall prepare himself to the battle?" (1 Corinthians 14:8.)

If only Paul could have felt the spirit of that conference! There was no evidence of uncertainty here. Rather there were clear, sharp, pointed, distinct instructions on the vital issues of the day and on the importance of the Latter-day Saints arising to the full measure of their callings and to the destiny that awaits them.

Latter-day Saints were told:

1. That they must live gospel principles or they would not be found worthy of the divine callings which they have received.

2. There can be no compromise with worldliness. We must be a "peculiar people" in the scriptural sense — peculiar in the eyes of those who do not keep the commandments of God; peculiar also in that they, as the Saints of God, put the Divine first in their lives. If that requires sacrifice, then sacrifice let it be. Haven't many others sacrificed for the gospel? Then why not this generation?

3. The sins of worldliness — if we submit to them — can shackle us and deter us from our divine destiny. Drunkenness, immorality, drug addiction, dishonesty, divorce, child neglect, all are satanic obstacles and devices deliberately conceived to destroy our effectiveness and our happiness.

4. The world is our field. The gospel is for everyone, Jew and gentile alike, in every land and clime. And who must take the good word to them? We must! We have the commission. We have the truth. We have the solemn and inescapable responsibility.

5. Such a program requires renewed strength and stability in the stakes and greater virility in the missions. All must recognize their responsibility to extend the kingdom of God, both at home and abroad.

6. Missionary work is the watchword, including "family-to-family" friendshipping as well as cooperation between members and missionaries. To preach the gospel is everyone's opportunity — yes, but more than that. It is everyone's duty, everyone's responsibility.

7. For young men, responding to missionary calls must be regarded as a part of their priesthood responsibility. All should live worthy lives, all should give this service. We are under covenant with God to do so.

President Kimball, with his clarion, clear and certain call, instructed us to lengthen our stride by becoming more devoted, more active, more productive.

Conversion is the secret of it all: self-conversion first, conversion within our own family group, and then conversion of all others who will give ear to the "trumpet's certain sound."

The Church is moving forward, but it must move faster and go farther. Since the whole world is our field, the whole world must be reached.

And President Kimball promised that with God's help we can do it!

FAITH AND FAITH ALONE?

An editorial in a widely circulated denominational newspaper carried a caption which said: "Salvation is by faith."

The first sentence of the editorial then read, "It must be by faith *alone,* because if salvation could come to us in any other way, then how could it be said to be by grace, and to what end did Christ die?"

Everyone of course who believes in the Savior will agree that salvation is by the grace of God, for without the free-will sacrifice of the Lord there would be no salvation.

Also, it will be generally agreed by most Christians that salvation must come by faith, for those who do not have faith in Christ will not serve him, and if they do not obey his commandments, again there is no salvation.

The difficulty with the "salvation by faith alone" concept is that its advocates lose sight of the actual purpose of the gospel. That purpose is not alone to be "saved," it is not merely to escape the flames of hell, and it is not even to live with the angels and sing praises and strum on harps throughout eternity.

The difficulty comes in misunderstanding the purpose of the gospel. That purpose is well expressed in the words of the Savior when he said: "Be ye therefore perfect, even as your Father which is in heaven is perfect." (Matthew 5:48.)

Our goal then is to become perfect like God; not like the angels, but like God! But how do we achieve such perfection? Through mere profession of faith? Through simply saying that we are "saved by grace" and letting it go at that?

We become perfect like God through obedience to the same principles which make him perfect. Obedience means work, and that means also that faith without the works of obedience is dead, regardless of all the professions we may make.

Works are dead without faith, and faith is equally dead without works. Our objective is not to become a part of the angelic choir; it goes far beyond that. *It is to become perfect like God our Father.*

That does not come by wishful thinking nor by pious professions alone. It comes by devoted hard work as well as by faith. We must be valiant in keeping commandments. We must build the kingdom. If we are not so valiant, we will never even see celestial glory. (D&C 76:79.)

Then to what end did Christ die? That we might become like our Father in heaven — perfect — through our applied faith and works.

SALVATION BY COMPROMISE?

Can we compromise our way into the kingdom of heaven? Many seem to think so, and therefore give token obedience to the commandments, but never actually submit fully to the Lord's requirements.

Can we go just halfway, and still receive our reward? The devil makes us think so, if he can, and tells us:

"Eat, drink, and be merry; nevertheless, fear God — he will justify in commiting a little sin; yea, lie a little, take the advantage of one because of his words, dig a pit for thy neighbor; there is no harm in this; and do all these things, for tomorrow we die: and if it so be that we are guilty, God will beat us with a few stripes, and at last we shall be saved in the kingdom of God." (2 Nephi 28:8.)

What a pity so many believe this devilish doctrine! With false teachings such as these, Lucifer induces many to cross over the line into his territory, persuading them that in fact they can serve two masters and still be saved.

The part-keeper of the Word of Wisdom, the part-keeper of the law of tithing, the part-keeper of the Sabbath Day, the social drinker, the part-keeper of other laws — all are in danger of slipping into the devil's trap.

The Lord will not allow us to pretend to serve him and the devil at the same time. We cannot be on both sides of the fence. We must be either for him or against him, and he has said that if we are not for him, we are, in fact, against him.

We cannot compromise with evil. God asks us to serve him with all our heart, might, mind and strength. The lukewarm he will not acknowledge.

BE GOOD AND DO GOOD

The gospel is not a passive way of life. It is active in every sense, even aggressive, although again it is the greatest expression of peace that we know.

The Lord commands that we shall be a good people. He expects us to be perfect, even as our Father which is in heaven is perfect, and we most certainly can begin on that path here and now. But even that requires that we *do* good things, that we *perform* in goodness, and that we *accomplish* the building of his kingdom.

Did he not say:

Do good to them that hate you.

Turn the other cheek.

Love even your enemies.

Pray for them that hate you.

Love your neighbor as yourself.

Love the Lord thy God.

Serve him.

Positive action is what he requires of us. It may be that we might be good even as we do nothing, but that is questionable. If we do nothing, do we not become regressive? A good car, if not used, can rust away. A good home, if not used, will deteriorate. A good man might do nothing and vegetate.

He commands us to be doers of the word and not hearers only. And as we become doers, it must be done with enthusiasm. Does he not command us to serve him with all our heart, all our might, all our mind, and all our strength?

One of the most important of all the commands by which we become doers is: "All things whatsoever ye would that men should do to you, do ye even so to them." (Matthew 7:12.) With it comes: Forgive men their trespasses.

And then there are the invitations he gives us wherein we must take the initiative:

Ask, and it shall be given you.

Seek, and ye shall find.

Knock and it shall be opened unto you.

And then:

Enter ye in at the strait gate. He will not come and push us in. We must take the step, we must put forth the effort, we must assume the initiative. And why? Because God will force no man to heaven.

"THINKETH NO EVIL"

The most famous words written by the apostle Paul are in the thirteenth chapter of 1 Corinthians. They have to do with charity and love. The Book of Mormon teaches that true charity is the pure love of Christ.

Without the love of Christ — true love for Christ and for our fellowmen — Paul said we are as nothing, even though we have all faith so that we could remove mountains or though we bestow all our goods to feed the poor.

Without true love of God and man, our piety is short indeed. This love for our fellowmen is so important. Paul said that the true love of Christ "thinketh no evil" and "rejoiceth not in iniquity." Think for a moment about that. What if no one thought evil thoughts; what if no one devised evil toward other people; what if our feet were not "swift in running to mischief"; what if we were never to sow discord; what if we never did deliberately lie or misrepresent; what if we never would steal or gossip or blacken another's name or bear false witness?

Paul was impressive when he said that true Christian love "rejoiceth not in iniquity." That is something to ponder over. If no one took joy in iniquity, would there be any iniquity?

Don't people sin because they think they will benefit by it? Isn't it the deception of Cain all over again — Cain who thought he could murder and get gain? Will not evil seed bring an evil harvest unfailingly? Dare we fall into Cain's delusion?

In the days of Adam, many of his children turned their backs upon the Lord for they loved Satan more than God. And why? Because they found joy in sin. They rejoiced in iniquity, and they allowed their minds to dwell on sin.

The thirteenth chapter of 1 Corinthians contains some of the most beautiful language in all holy writ. But it is more than that. It is a "job description" of a true follower of Christ, a divine formula for salvation.

How well do we fit into the pattern?

KINDNESS IS THE KEY

In the early revelations to the Prophet Joseph Smith, the Lord gave us a detailed description of what he expects of a Latter-day Saint. He specified the qualifications which he requires as follows:

Faith, hope and charity.

Love.

An eye single to the glory of God.

Faith, virtue and knowledge.

Temperance and patience.

Brotherly kindness.

Godliness.

Humility and diligence.

It is to be noted that he mentions kindness twice in his listing, as it appears in the fourth section of the Doctrine and Covenants. He likewise mentions charity twice.

Examine the list carefully, and see if kindness is not the key to them all.

How much faith in God does a cruel person have? How much hope in salvation can rest in his heart if he is unkind and uncharitable to his fellowmen? Can he have an eye single to God?

Can there be charity without kindness? The Book of Mormon defines true charity as the pure love of Christ and does it not tell us that without charity there is no salvation? (Ether 12:34.)

Can temperance and patience exist without kindness? Can there be brotherhood or sisterhood without it? And where is godliness without kindness?

Can there be genuine humility without a deep sense of affection and patience and understanding toward other people?

Kindness is the key.

It is no wonder that when the Lord gave us the Beatitudes he stressed the need of being merciful, peacemakers, and pure in heart. It is no wonder that he taught us to turn the other cheek, to go the extra mile, to give our coat and our cloak also.

Kindliness is next to godliness. Since the Savior is our pattern in life, let us never forget that he was kind.

SETTING OF PRIORITIES

Latter-day Saints must ever remember to put first things first. Priorities are all-important in every phase of life. Without establishing them, we would have little but chaos. Setting priorities requires organization on our part, proper planning of our affairs, and a good measure of self-discipline.

To establish the priorities of our lives, we must make up our minds to discover what is most important to us, and then chart a course to accomplish the purpose involved.

For us who believe in revelation from God, we have a sure word as to what is most important. It is not our selfish desires. In his own words the Lord has told us that it is seeking eternal life. He tells us that eternal life is the greatest gift of God to mankind (D&C 14:7), and he adds that he who has eternal life is rich. (D&C 6:7.)

Most people seek first for the riches and comforts of this world. They forget the eternal nature of their lives, that they are the children of God born in a pre-existent life, that mortality is but a brief period between the first eternity and the eternities that will follow mortality.

To allow the fleeting moment to blind us to the significance of the eternities is folly indeed. To allow our desire for the riches of this world to rob us of the riches of eternity is a blunder of unreal proportions.

The most important business of our lives should be to study and understand the gospel, obtain a testimony of it, and live its principles with all our "heart, might, mind and strength." (D&C 4:2.)

Relatively few people ever do this. The Savior knew that this condition would exist, but he nevertheless commands us to make the effort to be among the few. Said he:

"Enter ye in at the strait gate." Note that these words are given by way of commandment. "Enter ye in at the strait gate: for wide is the gate, and broad is the way, that leadeth to destruction, and many there be that go in thereat;

"Because strait is the gate, and narrow is the way, which leadeth unto life, and few there be that find it." (Matthew 7:13-14.)

And why do so few find it? Because their "hearts are set so much upon the things of this world." (D&C 121:35.)

Isn't it frightening to know that "few there be that find it"? Does it not persuade us to be numbered with the few?

Then should we not determine to accept this priority in our lives and follow the command of the Lord?

CAN WE BE PERFECT?

The Lord taught us to perfect our lives and he gave us the Church as a means toward that end. (Ephesians 4.) But is there really any perfection in mortality? Obviously it will require an eternity to be "perfect even as your Father which is in heaven is perfect," but the process can begin in this life. Otherwise, why would the Lord have commanded it?

List for yourself some of the commandments that we can keep perfectly even in this "veil of tears." It will be an enlightening experience. Here are a few:

Everyone can be perfect in refraining from the use of tobacco and liquor. Likewise, we can completely abstain from tea and coffee and other harmful things.

Everyone can pay a full tithing.

All can fast monthly as the Lord has commanded, and we can easily determine the value of the food thus saved and honestly contribute accordingly as a fast offering.

We can perfectly obey the advice of the Brethren to pray night and morning every day.

We can regularly observe family home evening as well as family prayer.

Barring sickness or other justifiable causes, we can regularly attend our meetings.

Everyone can be perfect in not profaning the name of Deity.

Every man can tell his wife every day that he loves her, and certainly wives can respond in kind.

Everyone can be perfect in keeping the law which says, "Thou shalt not steal."

We must be perfect in keeping the law against adultery.

Likewise we must not kill "nor do anything like unto it."

Every person can be perfect in not coveting another's husband or wife, or even his goods.

Everyone can observe the Sabbath day as the Lord has given it, if he really wants to.

And who needs to lie or cheat or bear false witness? Perfection in this regard is certainly within the reach of all. And so we might go on citing examples.

The Church is for the perfecting of the saints, said the apostle Paul, and we have the Church.

The gospel is free to all. The Church has its doors open to every soul. In it the Holy Ghost functions to guide us into all truth.

We individuals are the only uncertainties. But if we will hold to the Church and obey the truth, we can embark here and now on the way to perfection.

A GUIDING LIGHT

The ways of worldliness, even though they are increasingly evil, seem more and more to be the normal pattern of life, the acceptable things to do.

It is no wonder that the gospel seems like a bright ray of light amid the darkness. And so it must ever be to the true followers of Christ.

The gospel is light. It does dispel darkness. It truly is a radiant beacon showing us the way to go in these forbidding times. Likewise, each Latter-day Saint is a ray of light, for by his own righteous living he too becomes a beacon to his fellowmen.

As Elder Neal A. Maxwell, Assistant to the Twelve, has so effectively said, "This matter of being a light is even more important in dark times," and certainly we are living in a dark day of wickedness.

"Hence," said Elder Maxwell, "in these darkest hours, we must keep our individual lights shining. The moment of greatest danger is when there is so little light that darkness seems normal.

Church members can be models of morality, a glow of goodness like a perpetual midnight sun."

As he emphasized the need to keep our lights bright by our constant faithfulness to the Lord, he added:

"We must remember, however, that it is not necessary, either, that Satan extinguish our light, if he can simply keep it dim."

And how does he dim our lights? By persuading us to mere halfhearted effort in keeping the commandments; by salving our consciences by telling us that we can sin a little here and a little there and still be saved.

When we stay away from our meetings we dim our light. When we withhold our tithes and offerings, we dim our light. When we break the Word of Wisdom, when we profane, when we are dishonest, we dim our light. And when we submit to immorality, we come near to extinguishing it.

The Light of Christ is given to us freely if we will accept it, but when we turn our backs upon it, we are left in darkness indeed!

How vital are the words of the prophet Mormon:

"But whatsoever thing persuadeth men to do evil, and believe not in Christ, and deny him, and serve not God, then ye may know with a perfect knowledge it is of the devil; for after this manner doth the devil work, for he persuadeth no man to do good, no, not one; neither do his angels; neither do they who subject themselves unto him." (Moroni 7:17.)

And then we read in Mosiah: "If my people shall sow filthiness they shall reap the chaff thereof in the whirlwind." (Mosiah 7:30.)

THE DROP-OUTS

No one should risk his salvation by being a "drop-out" from true spirituality. The Lord has made this abundantly clear in his teachings. In fact his revelation on this subject is so specific that anyone knowing the truth should be afraid to withdraw from full participation in the kingdom of God.

What has the Lord said on this subject? In the Sermon on the Mount he gave a very enlightening but sobering expression:

"Ye are the salt of the earth: but if the salt have lost his savour, wherewith shall it be salted? it is thenceforth good for nothing, but to be cast out, and to be trodden under foot of men." (Matthew 5:13.)

Ponder upon that scripture in terms of persons who reject the truth, either by absenteeism, indifference, or open rebellion.

How do followers of Christ lose the savor of the salt? Is it not by disobedience, or neglect, or open rebellion against God? Is it not by accepting false philosophies and doctrines which are contrary to the revealed word? Is it not in resisting the authorized leaders of the Lord's kingdom, and refusing to sustain them?

What else has the Lord said?

"If ye continue in my word, then are ye my disciples indeed;

"And ye shall know the truth, and the truth shall make you free." (John 8:31, 32.)

If we continue in his word, dare we compromise with evil? If we fail to pay our tithes and offerings, if we violate the moral law, if we abuse the Sabbath, if we are dishonest, if we lie, or steal or cheat, do we continue in his word?

And if we do not continue in his word, are we really his disciples? If we are not really his disciples, are we not as salt that has lost its savor? And what does the rest of the scripture say?

In section 76 of the Doctrine and Covenants, as we read about those who fail to reach celestial glory but go to the terrestrial world instead, we find among them those who had the testimony of Jesus but were not valiant in it. (D&C 76:78-79.) If we are not valiant, are we his disciples indeed? If we are not valiant have we "lost our savor"?

There are those spoken of in section 132 who do not keep the commandments. He speaks of a certain group and says that they "did not abide my law; therefore, they cannot be enlarged, but remain separately and singly, without exaltation, in their saved condition, to all eternity." (D&C 132:17.)

Nothing is more clear than this from section 58: "He that doeth not anything until he is commanded, and receiveth a commandment with doubtful heart, and keepeth it with slothfulness, the same is damned." (D&C 58:29.)

It is not easy to enter the celestial kingdom. The Prophet Joseph said that if we enter there we must keep the celestial law, and the whole law too.

Who then can afford to be as salt that has lost its savor? Who can fail to be valiant? Who can hope for the reward without paying the price in devotion and obedience?

Why should anyone be content to be a "drop-out"?

"ADD TO YOUR FAITH"

The Lord has taught us to add to our faith, to build it up and to strengthen it. He has told us to learn by faith and to work by faith and to add important qualities of character to our faith.

One of his outstanding precepts is: "Add to your faith virtue."

The late Elder Richard L. Evans of the Council of the Twelve, one of our great advocates of a growing faith, expressed this thought: "Take your faith and add to it competence." What an interesting thought! And how important it is!

Every one of us should seek to serve the Lord in the most effective manner we can. In the Sermon on the Mount the Savior taught us to be perfect even as our Father in heaven is perfect.

The apostle Paul said that our leaders in the Church are for the perfecting of the saints and the edifying of the body of Christ.

We can and must develop skills in the Church, increased ability in carrying out its program, and greater effectiveness in teaching, visiting and influencing people to do right.

That is why we have a teachers' development program; that is why we have a bishops' training course; that is why we have monthly leadership meetings; that is why we outline our programs in well-prepared manuals; that is why we have stake conferences and ward conferences and the general conferences of the Church and of its auxiliaries and priesthood organizations.

"Add to your faith competence." Then, and only then, can we really serve God with all our heart, might, mind and strength. Only then are we truly valiant in the work and anxiously engaged in the good cause.

WE MUST EXERCISE IT!

"What shall we do with faith?" asked Elder LeGrand Richards one day. And this courageous member of the Council of the Twelve answered in only two words: "Exercise it."

There is no other answer. Without such exercise, faith dies. And how do we exercise it? With righteous works in obedience to the commandments of God.

The ancient writer James was not the only one who taught that faith without works is dead. The Prophet Joseph was just as emphatic, saying at one time: "Will the mere admission that this is the will of heaven ever benefit us if we do not comply with all of its teachings? Do we not offer violence to the Supreme Intelligence of heaven when we admit the truth of its [the Bible] teachings and not obey them?"

The Lord was most emphatic. He plainly taught that professions of faith alone will not save, for not everyone that cries out to him shall enter the kingdom, but only those who do the will of his Father in heaven.

In modern revelation the Lord stated it so well:

"Men should be anxiously engaged in a good cause. . . .

"But he that doeth not anything until he is commanded, and receiveth a commandment with a doubtful heart, and keepeth it with slothfulness, the same is damned." (D&C 58:27, 29.)

And he added that only the valiant in the testimony of Jesus shall wear the crown over the kingdom. (D&C 76:78-79.)

PREPARATION NEEDED

The response of the Church to the appeal of President Kimball for more missionaries has been remarkable from every standpoint. The loyalty of the people to their leader is indeed commendable.

The youth of the Church are responding far and wide; the urge to fill missions is increasing, and is a splendid evidence of the faith of our young people.

This is true in other countries as well as in the United States and Canada, from whence most of the missionaries have come in the past. It is interesting to note that for many years more than half of the missionaries have come from the state of Utah alone. But the picture is now changed. Countries other than the United States and Canada now are sending nearly half of the total number.

President Kimball indeed was inspired when he appealed to people in other lands to provide their own missionaries. It will be a bright day indeed when each country can furnish its own quota to labor among its own people, having the language, and knowing the local customs.

That will in turn leave the American missionaries for new fields to be opened as the missionary enterprise extends to other nations not as yet reached.

In an address given by President Ezra Taft Benson of the Council of the Twelve at the April 1975 general conference, he pointed up the great need for preparation of missionaries before they enter the field. Among other things he said: "We need missionaries to match our message."

Our message is so meaningful and so vital to the welfare of all peoples that it must be presented in the most effective way. Such a presentation requires a deep conversion on the part of the missionary himself so that he may bear an unswerving testimony of the truth of the work. But it also requires a full acquaintance with the gospel so that its principles may be explained in simplicity and accuracy.

And where shall such preparation take place? In the home and in our meetings. Every home with boys should plant in the hearts of their growing young men a love for the truth, with a desire to teach it as the young men reach the proper age.

With conversion will come desire — a desire to serve. But it rests largely in the hands of the parents who must teach, provide the proper home atmosphere and set the necessary example in their own lives. It is verily true that as the twig is bent, so will grow the tree.

Class leaders, priesthood advisers and ward and branch officials must realize that it is their responsibility as well as their opportunity to fulfill their part in this program. They too must bend every effort to see that we have "missionaries to match our message."

Missionaries called within foreign lands often have little with which to support themselves. Contributions to the First Presidency's missionary fund assist them in their need. This too is a way in which we may further provide "missionaries to match our message."

THE TIME TO ACT

Following each general conference, the members of the Church have opportunity to consider carefully — or forget — the words of their leaders. Whether they consider or forget will have a significant effect upon their future lives.

It has been the history of the past that many people have decided to forget the conferences and their messages. They have been filled with fervor or have been emotionally built up for the moment, but then have silently dropped back into their former routine.

That should not happen. Can we not feel an urgency about present-day conditions? Do we not feel a part of what is going on around us? Can we not sense that we have a special situation to deal with, in that we have been given a divine commission by the Almighty which is pertinent *now,* and that this calling will not only affect our own lives but likewise those of many others who need our message?

This is a day of warning, the Lord has declared. And who are to give this warning? *We are.* We cannot escape it. It is our lot, our commission, and our calling.

To live the gospel here at home in a spirit of contentment, more or less forgetting the world's need for our message, is no way to be Latter-day Saints.

We are not a passive people, nor should we be. We must not be an idle people, either, so far as the Lord's work is concerned. The Lord said the idler should be cast out.

We must aggressively move forward with the Lord's program, and that forward movement must begin with each individual. It will be remembered that Sister Jessie Evans Smith used to sing:

"Let there be peace on earth, and let it begin with me." It is that philosophy which we now must adopt with respect to our responsibility to the Lord and to the world. If we are to save others, let us start by first putting our own house in order.

That is why President Spencer W. Kimball, in his closing remarks at the April 1975 conference, said: "This is the day of repentance, a day for people to take stock of their situations and to change their lives where necessary."

Let us gird for the battle of righteousness. Each must do as the apostle Paul told the Ephesians:

"Take unto you the whole armour of God, that ye may be able to withstand in the evil day. . . . having your loins girt about with truth, and having on the breastplate of righteousness: And your feet shod with the preparation of the gospel of peace; Above all, taking the shield of faith. . . . and . . . the helmet of salvation, and the sword of the Spirit, which is the word of God." (Ephesians 6:13-17.)

Can we do less? The trumpet has sounded a clear and certain call. As the soldiers of God, we must respond aggressively, but humbly, with "all [our] heart, might, mind and strength, that [we] may stand blameless before God at the last day." (D&C 4:2.)

4.

LAW AND OBEDIENCE

LET US PRACTICE IT

When the Prophet Joseph Smith wrote the Articles of Faith he included this very well known one:

"We believe in being subject to kings, presidents, rulers, and magistrates, in obeying, honoring, and sustaining the law."

The Doctrine and Covenants sets forth these basic principles:

"We believe that governments were instituted of God for the benefit of man; and that he holds men accountable for their acts in relation to them, both in making laws and administering them, for the good and safety of society.

"We believe that no government can exist in peace, except such laws are framed and held inviolate as will secure to each individual the free exercise of conscience, the right and control of property, and the protection of life.

"We believe that all governments necessarily require civil officers and magistrates to enforce the laws of the same; and that such as will administer the law in equity and justice should be sought for and upheld by the voice of the people if a republic, or the will of the sovereign." (D&C 134:1-3.)

These basic principles should be kept in mind now as never before. In every land, law and order can be achieved and maintained only on these principles.

Since these teachings are doctrine with the Latter-day Saints, and since they form a part of our modern scripture, every member of the Church in every land should conform to these principles, remembering that the Lord has also said:

"Let no man break the laws of the land, for he that keepeth the laws of God hath no need to break the laws of the land." (D&C 58:21.)

He then taught that members of his Church must be subject to the powers that be until the Savior comes to institute his millennial rule.

Election campaigns in the United States are vigorous and sometimes bitter. The citizens then cast their votes and the majority of course rules. There is both rejoicing and disappointment over the election, depending on where individual allegiance happens to lie.

But regardless of any person's private notions concerning the outcome of any election, he should — if he is a Latter-day Saint — follow the divine principles laid down by the Prophet Joseph Smith and our modern scriptures.

"Wherefore, be subject to the powers that be," as the Lord indicates. "He that keepeth the laws of God hath no need to break the laws of the land." This is part of our gospel teaching. It should be put into practice in everyone's life. Making professions is not enough. We must practice what we preach.

THE VALUE OF LAWS

It has been said very frequently that obedience is the first law of heaven. Whether it is or not probably doesn't matter, because all of God's laws are important, and who can say that one has any priority over another?

But whether obedience is first or not, it is nevertheless basic, for without it there is no salvation, no progress, no real happiness, and no return to the presence of God, there to live with him in eternity.

Actually, without obedience there is no happiness in this life either, and no progress and no security. So obedience is really basic, and those who choose to be otherwise do themselves inestimable harm.

The Lord said: "That which is governed by law is also preserved by law and perfected and sanctified by the same." (D&C 88:34.)

What a choice statement this is! How carefully it should be pondered!

And then the Lord said in the following verse: "That which breaketh a law, and abideth not by law, but seeketh to become a law unto itself, and willeth to abide in sin, . . . cannot be sanctified by law, neither by mercy, justice, nor judgment. Therefore, they must remain filthy still."

This is a vital message for every person. Most right-thinking people believe in God. Most of them also believe in a hereafter and hope to spend eternity in the presence of God. But do they think of the significance of these few lines of scripture?

There is only one way to become sanctified and perfected, and thus prepared to live with God. That is by obedience to his laws. There is no other way. Being governed by law preserves us, protects us, perfects us and sanctifies us. But refusing to be governed by law has just the opposite effect. It leaves us "filthy still."

And what of those who just give lip service, who appear to obey but in reality do not? Such, the Lord says, he will spew out of his mouth, which no one should relish. (Revelation 3:15-16.)

When will we learn to obey him with all our heart, might, mind and strength? If we really hope for salvation, we must earn it.

REAPING THE WHIRLWIND

In our earliest days at school we learned the lessons of cause and effect. We struck a ball and it moved. We obstructed its movement and it stopped. We put a stick in a hot fire and it burned. We turned an electric switch and light appeared. It all seemed very simple. The lesson was thorough and undeviating. We could readily see its truth.

Cause and effect are also part of life in general. We obey the law and we live as peaceful citizens. We disobey and we are apprehended. We live the laws of health and we ward off illness. We abuse our bodies and become ill.

It is so morally also. As we break the moral law many afflictions come upon us; some are crippling, some cause blindness, some bring insanity and some death. All bring unhappiness.

But we never seem to learn life's lessons. Many think they have fun in self-abuse. Drunkenness to the drinker is not abhorrent. It is socially acceptable in certain circles. It is said that the majority of Americans drink — socially at least — because it is "the thing to do." They forget the law of cause and effect.

Jesus came into the world offering the abundant life. Few believed him. But in our day, when the gospel has been restored and we can see its fruits in our own lives and in the lives of our friends, we see that indeed it provides the abundant life for those who obey its teachings.

And for those who do not obey? Its blessings are withheld. In this life, we reap as we sow; the good tree will bring forth good fruit and the bad tree produces only bad. The contrasts are great. Blessings follow obedience, but in disobedience we reap the whirlwind.

An ancient teaching of the Lord should be profitable today. It is as binding now as it was when it was given through Moses:

"Behold, I set before you this day a blessing and a curse;

"A blessing if ye obey the commandments of the Lord your God, which I command you this day;

"And a curse, if ye will not obey the commandments of the Lord your God, but turn aside out of the way which I command you this day." (Deuteronomy 11:26-27, 28.)

It is as simple as that. We grow only as we apply the rules of growth. Retrogression is the direct result of disobedience. As Joshua told his people, we may choose whom we shall serve, and thereby learn what our reward will be.

CORRECT PRINCIPLES

Most Latter-day Saints will remember that the Prophet Joseph Smith was asked at one time how he governed his people. His reply was that he taught them correct principles and they then governed themselves.

This oft-quoted statement of the Prophet contains a wealth of wisdom. It relates directly of course to the principle of free agency which the Lord has given to all mankind. It follows the plan of the Savior, who always taught correct principles and allowed his hearers to conduct themselves accordingly. As our hymn so beautifully says:

"He'll call, persuade, direct aright,
And bless with wisdom, love and light,
In nameless ways be good and kind,
But never force the human mind."

We are taught the various principles of correct living; we are given the law of virtue; we are taught to be honest, to live the Word of Wisdom, the law of tithing, principles related to saving our dead, and various other great precepts.

None is compelled to observe the teachings. All have perfect free agency with respect to them. The blessings of the Church come to those who keep the commandments; they are not enjoyed by the disobedient.

As the Book of Mormon teaches with respect to the atonement of the Savior: we receive of his redemption if we obey him; if we are disobedient, it is the same as if no redemption had been made.

This principle of teaching correct doctrines and allowing us to govern ourselves as we like, either in obedience or disobedience, relates likewise to our associations with other people.

Most of the Sermon on the Mount is devoted to our dealings with others; it is so also with the Ten Commandments. The second great commandment teaches us to love our neighbors as ourselves, as does the Golden Rule. But we are not compelled to do unto others as we would be done by; we still have our free agency.

The same is true with respect to the laws of the land. We teach observance, but there are still those who feel free to rob banks, steal from stores, and violate speed limits.

We should take part in proper community affairs, because we need good community conditions in which to rear our families. In such undertakings, neighbors and citizens may well join together; but many choose otherwise

There is our interest in public elections too. Here again every person has his agency. He is free to support any party or any candidate, and the Church does not interfere. Again, we are to govern ourselves.

A two-party system in politics is all-important. If there were only one party, we would have dictatorship and meaningless elections. The two-party system provides for right of choice and free agency. We protect this system, therefore, and seek to encourage good people to be active in both parties, urging good men to become candidates in both. This provides for good government by good people. But always free agency prevails. No one is forced to belong to any party or group; all have the right of choice.

The principle laid down by the Prophet Joseph is inherent in our religion, and all should hold fast to it. We will learn correct principles and conduct ourselves accordingly.

DOING UNTO OTHERS

There is more than at first "greets the eye" in the Golden Rule. This commandment is as basic as the Resurrection and as essential to salvation as faith itself. Examine it for a moment:

"All things whatsoever ye would that men should do to you, do ye even so to them." (Matthew 7:12.)

Is there a greater law of human relationships than that? It applies to business, to family associations, to recreation — to any and all phases of life. If we would get along well with other people, we must do unto them as we would be done by.

This is equally true: If we would get along well with God, we must do unto other people as we would be done by, and also do unto God as we would have him do unto us.

Read the Ten Commandments. Every one relates either to our attitude toward God or to our actions toward other people.

If we should do unto others as we would be done by, would there be any crime, any stealing, lying, coveting, adultery or murder? Would there be any assaults on another's person? Would there be any war?

If we lived this law would there be any intrigue in business, government or politics? Would any homes be broken up? Would there be family quarrels?

The second great commandment directs that we love our neighbors as ourselves. Can we keep this commandment without also keeping the Golden Rule, and if we do not keep the Golden Rule, can we keep this second great commandment? And if we do not keep this second commandment, can we claim to keep the first — to love the Lord with our whole heart and soul?

We are living in a sinful world and wickedness is multiplying rapidly. One of the fastest-spreading of all sins is dishonesty. Consider that one point for a moment. It is one of the most widespread of all violations of the Golden Rule. It is the root of the violation of at least half of the Ten Commandments.

Then may we ask if any Christian, or any believer in God at all, can ever hope for salvation without honesty?

The same thing is true of unkindness. It too is deeply involved in the Golden Rule. Can any unkind person (who therefore certainly does not love his neighbor as himself) ever enter the kingdom of Heaven without a great deal of repentance?

Can any dishonest person — without complete repentance — ever come into the presence of him who said that no unclean thing can enter the kingdom? Are not both unkindness and dishonesty unclean and reprehensible? Is there anything Christlike about them?

Speaking of the Golden Rule, the Savior said: "This is the law and the prophets." Speaking of the two great commandments, he said: "On these two commandments hang all the law and the prophets." Can there be any salvation without them?

We can very readily measure our own qualifications for salvation by simply determining how well we keep these commandments.

Certainly in this matter we may well understand that faith without works is dead.

FOR OUR SECURITY

One of the principal worries of most people is their security for the future.

We have social security, insurance programs, and retirement plans, not to mention the "cradle to the grave" security proposals that constantly raise their heads.

Where is solid security?

With inflation now a serious problem throughout the world, we have many memories of the Great Depression following the Wall Street tragedy of 1929. Money wasn't worth much after that.

How many remember the value of German money following the war? One meal in a cafe cost a million marks.

Where is security? Is it in "the arm of flesh" or had we better look elsewhere?

Of course we should have security in insurance and retirement programs. In times like these, they are indispensable. It would be foolhardy to be without them. But thoughtful people look deeper than such matters. Security without fear needs to come from elsewhere. It is of greater value than money, or armies or navies. What is it?

When the prophet Lehi blessed his son Joseph he promised him "security forever," but with a strong condition: "if it so be that ye shall keep the commandments of the Holy One of Israel." (2 Nephi 3:2.)

The Book of Mormon is filled with promises of security to the Lord's people if they will but obey his commandments. Similar promises are made in the Bible. Note this one in particular:

"If ye walk in my statutes, and keep my commandments, and do them;

"Then I will give you rain in due season, and the land shall yield her increase and the trees of the field shall yield their fruit.

"And your threshing shall reach unto the vintage, and the vintage shall reach unto the sowing time: and ye shall eat your bread to the full, and dwell in your land safely.

"And I will give you peace in the land, and ye shall lie down, and none shall make you afraid: and I will rid evil beasts out of the land, neither shall the sword go through your land.

"For I will have respect unto you, and make you fruitful, and multiply you, and establish my covenant with you." (Leviticus 26:3-6, 9.)

What more could any people ask? Is there better security than that?

On the other hand, the Lord declared, "If ye will not hearken unto me, and will not do all these commandments; And if ye shall despise my statutes. . . . I will set my face against you." (Leviticus 26:14, 15, 17.) He then tells the result of such an act in the rest of this same chapter of Leviticus.

We put up with drought and business failures, with wars and crime, but never turn to the source of real relief from these conditions. Are we really as bright as we sometimes think we are?

DAYS OF VIOLENCE

What can we do to fight the violence which seems to sweep this and almost every other nation? Careful observers fear that we shall be engulfed by crime within another decade. Thoughtful people are becoming frightened at its increase, and well they may, for in it are the seeds of utter chaos, even of the destruction of civilization.

Too often we look upon violence as something which only affects the other fellow, or as something which is native to the underworld but not a part of the better side of society. This is a fallacy. Corruption is invading the best of circles and the highest categories in our society. Dishonesty has reached into the very heart of our social structure. If it is not checked and reversed, we cannot survive as a civilized race.

The Lord has firmly warned America through the Book of Mormon. Its pages are replete with evidences of the destruction of the people as they depart from righteousness. The warning is blunt and direct: The inhabitants of this land must either repent and serve God, or be destroyed.

But who are the violent ones? The criminals? They certainly are, heaven knows. But what others are violent? Would we be shocked to realize that every person who violates the law and the Lord's divine precepts is a violator, a lawbreaker, to that degree?

If we violate the rules of right and justice, are we ourselves "violent" in that respect. And if we who profess to be law-abiding citizens tolerate even a little violation on our own part, can we blame others who are worse than we are?

There is a song which says: "Let there be peace on earth, and let it begin with me." We all might well adopt that thinking and say: "Let there be an end to violence, and let it begin with me."

Strong individuals can build strong families. Strong families can build strong communities, and virile communities can make a powerful nation.

If each individual would cease to steal, cease to lie, cease to cheat; if each of us would stop lustful practices, selfishness and covetousness, we would take a mighty step toward eliminating violence altogether.

When it is realized, for example, that a large percentage of men, women and children in America are shoplifters, costing the nation billions of dollars each year, does it not bring the problem close to home?

If we want violence to end in this country, we had better begin in each home with each family and each individual. That would be the leaven in the lump. If such action were to multiply and spread as fast as shoplifting has spread, we would make a glorious beginning toward national peace and security.

THE TEN COMMANDMENTS

The Ten Commandments have formed the basis of good conduct ever since they were first given. So important are they that the Lord has repeated them from time to time.

The most recent such instances appear in sections 42, 58 and 59 of the Doctrine and Covenants. They merit frequent study.

The listing provided by Nephi in the Book of Mormon is an interesting one. As is the case with the revelations in the Doctrine and Covenants, Nephi provides some variation, but the divine principles are there in great plainness, never varying. Said he:

"Men should not murder.

"They should not lie.

"They should not steal.

"They should not take the name of the Lord their God in vain.

"They should not envy.

"They should not have malice.

"They should not contend one with another.

"They should not commit whoredoms.

"They should do none of these things; for whoso doeth them shall perish." (2 Nephi 26:32.)

Nephi also strongly urged against priestcrafts: "For, behold, priestcrafts are that men preach and set themselves up for a light unto the world, that they may get gain and praise of the world; but they seek not the welfare of Zion." (2 Nephi 26:29.)

He likewise taught that all men should have charity, which is the love of Christ, without which there is no salvation. (2 Nephi 26:30.)

There is no escaping the basics in the gospel. They need constant consideration, reconsideration and never-ending application, for without them, what have we?

"THIS IS THE LAW"

When the Savior gave the first and second great commandments, he said of them: "On these two commandments hang all the law and the prophets." (Matthew 22:40.) Since he included both the law of Moses and the teachings of the prophets, he made these two requirements all-inclusive. The whole gospel rests upon them.

At another time he gave a further interpretation of the second great commandment as he taught the Golden Rule. He said: "All things whatsoever ye would that men should do to you, do ye even so to them," and, "for this is the law and the prophets." (Matthew 7:12.)

The law of Moses was given as a schoolmaster to bring the ancients up to Christian standards, according to the apostle Paul. Therefore, of necessity the law had to reflect the gospel teachings of the prophets, although in a rudimentary way.

If this were not so it would not teach its lesson and its end would never be accomplished. Thus, both the law and the prophets emphasized the basic principle of doing to others as one would be done by. Then came the later teaching: "He that loveth not his brother whom he hath seen, how can he love God whom he hath not seen? And this commandment have we from him, That he who loveth God love his brother also." (1 John 4:20, 21.)

Is it any wonder then that Paul wrote: "Faith, hope, charity, these three; but the greatest of these is charity"? (1 Corinthians 13:13.)

It is not surprising either, therefore, that Moroni taught that unless we have charity we cannot inherit the kingdom of heaven. (Ether 12:34.)

Then dare any Christian be hateful, or vengeful, or unkind?

FULL OR PART OBEDIENCE?

Where do you expect to spend eternity? That was the topic advertised for discussion at a recent religious gathering. The speaker talked of heaven and hell. He said we all have a choice. Where we go is up to us. This was the theme of his sermon. And much of what he said is true.

We do have a choice. We can have any kind of eternity we want, in heaven or hell or in many of the available places in between.

It is good to ask ourselves: Where are we going to spend eternity? We can tell quite easily, for the Lord has spelled it out rather plainly.

To go to the celestial kingdom, we must be "valiant" in the testimony of Jesus. (D&C 76:79.) If we are not, we will go to the terrestrial kingdom. It remains for us to define "valiant" in the Lord's terms. How does he explain it?

To be valiant, he says, we must serve him with "all [our] heart, might, mind and strength." (D&C 4:2.)

We must "be anxiously engaged in a good cause" and "bring to pass much righteousness." (D&C 58:27.)

We must learn our duty and act in the office to which we are appointed "in all diligence." (D&C 107:99.)

The Prophet Joseph said that if we hope to attain celestial glory we must live the celestial law "and the *whole* law too."

Where will we spend eternity?

FREEDOM OF RELIGION

One of the dearest possessions of the free peoples of the world is the right to worship God according to the dictates of their own conscience. Wars have been fought over this principle. It is a basic tenet of the United States Constitution. Free agency is so vital to Christianity that there would be no gospel without it.

The Lord will never force us. We can worship him or ignore him or defy him as we please. He will not interfere. But dear as religious freedom is, we still must remember that there is a right and a wrong, even to religion, and that whereas God will allow us to be wrong if we desire so to be, nevertheless, he himself holds strictly to one "strait and narrow way."

Freedom of religion gives us permission to join any church we like, or to belong to no church at all, just as free agency allows us to sin or not, according to our wishes.

But freedom of religion does not allow us to alter the doctrines of God, and to suppose that our man-made alterations will provide us with salvation. We must follow the plan of the Lord if we wish his blessings. How clearly he explained this when he said: "In vain they do worship me, teaching for doctrines the commandments of men." (Matthew 15:9.)

Some content themselves by sitting back complacently and telling themselves that this applies to the other fellow; that "we are in the true Church so we need not worry." But it applies to everyone.

Jude of old urged the saints to "earnestly contend for the faith which was once delivered unto the saints." (Verse 3.) In his day people were leaving that faith. Some were confused by false teachings, but others simply became careless and discontinued devoted adherence to the principles of the gospel in their daily lives.

Are we like those ancient saints? Do we need to examine our own lives in terms of the "faith which was once delivered unto the saints"?

Where do we stand on Sabbath observance, chastity, or the Word of Wisdom? where on tithing, fasting and fast offerings, attendance at meetings, honesty, and the Golden Rule?

It would surprise a great many of us were we to measure our attitudes and practices against the detailed requirements of the "faith which was once delivered unto the saints."

GODLESSNESS VERSUS LIBERTY

Since freedom is a gift of heaven, can we preserve it by violating the very law upon which it is predicated? Can we hope to retain the blessings of liberty by ignoring him who is the Author of liberty?

Do we suppose that we can go on in our godless practices and receive continued mercy from the Being whom we offend?

As lovers of liberty, we must recognize the source from whence this blessing comes. We must purge from our hearts the unbelief which daily loosens our grasp on the very principles for which we send our sons to war. We must believe that God lives, and that he is a power to be reckoned with, regardless of ignorance or prejudice.

This fact some have learned through bitter experience. It was a truth which Moses impressed upon the children of Israel in his day. To the assembled hosts in the wilderness, eagerly awaiting admittance to the Promised Land, he said:

"Behold, I set before you this day a blessing and a curse;

"A blessing, if ye obey the commandments of the Lord your God, which I command you this day:

"And a curse, if ye will not obey the commandments of the Lord your God, but turn aside out of the way which I command you this day." (Deuteronomy 11:26-28.)

If the people of America will serve the Lord and keep his commandments, and thereby nurture the spirit of freedom, we will be blessed and prospered, and this country will go on to a glorious destiny.

If we follow in his footsteps, we shall never have need to fear for the safety of our cities or farms, our industries or our homes, for he will strengthen us as he did the armies of ancient Israel, and bring us victory.

OUR SUNDAY HABITS

What is the purpose of the Sabbath day? Is it a day for rest alone, or for relaxation and recreation? Or does it have a deeper meaning?

There are many who just "rest" on the Sabbath, and who seldom if ever attend church services; but they do read Sunday papers, watch TV, eat heavy dinners, and nap on the front room couch. Is this what the Lord expects?

And there are many who golf or ski on Sunday, or fish or hunt and come home tired at night to sleep and thus recoup their energies. Have they pleased the Lord?

One man said: "Sunday is just a day of rest, and the important thing is to get some relaxation and rest from the normal routine."

Another said: "If going to church is unpleasant, stay away."

And still another: "Sunday is no different from Monday in the eyes of the Lord. Do on Sunday what you would do on Monday."

Views such as those are what have made Sunday a day of fun and recreation for much of the world and drawn them away from the Lord. But is that God's idea of the Sabbath?

The Lord did set apart the Sabbath from Mondays and all other days. He did call it "my holy day." He did declare it a day of rest, but he did not stop there, for he made it a day of worship as well. He made it a time for building his kingdom.

It is just as much a violation of the Sabbath to refuse to worship as it is to resume our usual employment on that day. It is just as much a violation of the Sabbath to spend the day in recreation as to spend it in making money.

Sunday is for rest — *plus* — and that plus includes going to the house of prayer "on my holy day" and there offering up our sacraments and oblations to the Lord, confessing our sins to our brethren and making the necessary upward adjustment in our lives. It includes building the kingdom of God by our good works.

Rest alone on the Sabbath is a violation of the spirit of the Sabbath. Skiing and similar activities on Sunday are violations of the Sabbath. Failure to attend church services without a reasonable excuse is a violation of both the law and the spirit of the Sabbath. Failure to truly worship God on that day is a violation of the principle of Sabbath observance.

Sunday should be given over to sincere worship of the Lord, to building his kingdom, to increasing our faith, to teaching our children the principles of the gospel, to bringing about closer family solidarity, to making reconciliation with those whom we have offended (this before we "bring our gift to the altar"), and to "keeping ourselves unspotted from the sins of the world."

What else did the Lord say? "And on this day thou shalt do none other thing, only let thy food be prepared with singleness of heart." (D&C 59:13.)

If we are sincere followers of the Savior, we do not have the option of doing anything that pleases our vanity on his holy day, for he has commanded us in firm language what we are to do, and that is to worship him.

THE LORD'S FRANKNESS

It is a testimony indeed to read the Lord's frank discussion with the Prophet Joseph Smith at the time Martin Harris took the 116 pages of Book of Mormon manuscript. The manner in which the Lord reasoned with Joseph shows the matter-of-fact approach the Lord takes to problems, and how practical indeed he is. (D&C 10.)

Joseph at this time was only twenty-three years old. He was unlettered and unschooled, and not sophisticated in the ways of the world, but the Lord knew what was afoot among his enemies, and frankly but kindly told the boy prophet what dangers confronted him.

It is good to know how practical the Lord actually is. It is good to know that he can be practical with us, as well as with Joseph Smith, and that if we will but trust him as Joseph did, he will respond to our needs.

As the Creator of all things, he knows about all things, and he knows well the thinking and planning — evil as well as good — of men. We should feel greatly comforted, therefore, in placing ourselves in his hands. All he requires of us is that we serve him and keep his commandments, for this is the whole duty of man. (Ecclesiastes 12:13.)

WALKING WITH GOD

The soloist sang his beautiful number in church and repeated in his song the expression, "I'll walk with God." Following the service, as he went home alone, he began to review in his mind the words of the number he had presented so well: "I'll walk with God."

The more he reflected upon it, the more he questioned whether he himself really walked with God. What did it mean to walk with the Almighty?

He recalled that actually and physically some of the ancient prophets had walked and talked with him. God is a Personage, like any other personage in form, because man was made in his image. Therefore, of course, one personage could walk and talk with another.

As he studied the matter in his mind, however, he felt sure that this was not what the writer of the song had in mind.

Can people "walk with God" now, even though they may not be privileged to do so physically? May we walk with him in the sense that his Spirit will be with us and about us and guide and comfort us? Was that what the composer of the song meant?

The ancients who walked with God "as one man with another," were men who were fully acceptable to him. They were pure; they were obedient; they were in harmony with the Almighty. If we walk with God today, then, even in the spiritual sense, must we not be as pure and obedient as they were?

The singer asked himself, "Do I walk with God if I violate the Sabbath day?" He had to admit that the answer was no.

"If I take the name of the Lord in vain, do I walk with God?"

"If I am not clean morally, do I walk with God?"

"If I am dishonest, and fail to do to others as I would be done by, do I walk with him?"

"If I do not love my neighbor as myself, do I walk with him?"

"What about tithing, the Word of Wisdom, church attendance, sustaining our leaders? Do they enter into the question?"

As he reached home from the service he was quite convinced that we walk with God only if we obey him. The Lord would hardly tolerate our company otherwise, for no unclean thing can come into his presence.

5.

SIN

AND

SOCIETY

A PERMISSIVE SOCIETY

The *News-Chronicle* of Vallejo, California, once carried an article written by Delores Skinner, quoting Charles Muchel, chief of police for the nearby city of Fairfield, California.

The chief was addressing a meeting of the North Solano Retired Officers Association and, as Miss Skinner expressed it, "He didn't pull any punches, and it was refreshing to hear some of his comments on this permissive society and what the lack of discipline is doing to those who live in it."

He branded as cruel the inattention of parents to the rearing of their children; he called permissiveness misguided and added that "thousands of young people in the past several years have been allowed to commit crime after crime and grow into confirmed criminals practically without any organized effort to stop them.

"This overemphasis on the permissiveness point of view flies in the face of all the wisdom of the ages concerning the effective upbringing of children. This thinking has infiltrated the criminal justice system and recently has brought a negative public reaction; even, perhaps understandably, an overreaction to its resulting policies," he said.

The current belief among many is that to enter a person into the criminal justice system will be harmful, he said, emphasizing the fact that he believed that rehabilitation is a justified goal and morally right, but he added, "There is no logic in eliminating discipline or punishment."

Most successful people, the speaker noted, have one common characteristic — self-discipline — while the common thread running through the criminal element is the absence of discipline, or a "me first" adolescent attitude.

Children are crying out to parents for direction and this direction cannot be given by abdicating parental responsibility and expecting schools or churches to do what is not only the parents' right but their obligation, he continued.

A lack of spiritual and moral training by loving parents, he pointed out, is the "single cause of problem children today."

Law enforcement officers from one end of the country to another, from small hamlets to the FBI, all tell the same story, but they are like a "voice crying in the wilderness." Will the nation wake up to their warning?

The whole matter reminds one of a stirring quotation from the Book of Mormon: "If the time comes that the voice of the people doth choose iniquity, then is the time that the judgments of God will come upon you." (Mosiah 29:27.)

Is our widespread public apathy and indifference to permissiveness and lack of discipline to be interpreted as the voice of the people? For the good of all concerned, let us hope otherwise.

THE EVIL OF VULGARITY

As the world has grown more wicked in recent years, human beings have become more and more vulgar in their habits and in their thinking.

Vulgarity is defined as that which is coarse, unwholesome, indecent, indelicate, ill-mannered, dishonest, unclean and unchaste. It lives with profanity and thrives on filth. It is marked by dirty talk, unkempt appearance, and questionable conduct.

Many people have now descended into the depths of vulgarity and as they revel in filth they try to impose their wicked ways on the rest of us. The time is long since past when we should fight this plague with all the righteous power within our reach, and we have an infinite amount of that power if we will only tap its divine reservoir.

Why do so many of us remain silent while vulgarity corrupts our sons and daughters?

Why do we allow evil and violent television and radio programs, pornographic magazines and books to invade our homes and there upset the ideals we have established for our families?

Why do we allow many of our young people to suppose — without correction — that moral standards have changed and that now anything goes?

Are we to allow seductive influences to wipe out our concept of virtue?

These evils cover a wide range. What is behind the craze for rock music, for example? It is sin and vulgarity. What gives rise to immodest dress? It is sin and vulgarity.

Why do some young people in many areas deliberately dress like tramps and hippies? It is because worldliness has made vulgarity popular, causing these young people to become so confused in their values that they think the seamy side of life is desirable.

Vulgarities of today have led to a lowering of nearly all standards of conduct. It has always been vulgar to neck and pet, to challenge virtue, to drink, to steal, to cheat, to lie, to tell filthy stories.

But, sad to say, among many people it is no longer so. Many actually think it is smart to lie and to deceive; they regard it as a conquest when they can overcome righteous objections and tempt a boy or a girl to lose their virtue. It is a conquest, true enough, of evil over good, but it is diabolical.

Experts who have studied it repeatedly blame parents for the condition, many of whom, themselves, have become vulgar.

To cure this epidemic, we must come back to the family circle, bring the gospel and its high ideals into every home, and not be ashamed of it, for it is indeed the power of God unto salvation, in the home and out, and especially now in this evil day.

HOW GREAT IS THAT SIN?

In this day of the "new morality," as sex permissiveness is called, it is well for all to read again what the Lord has said about the violation of the moral law. If people choose to go into such sin, they should have their eyes open to the seriousness of it, and the eventual penalty if they fail to repent.

The prophet Alma, as is well known, told his son that in the eyes of the Lord only murder and sin against the Holy Ghost are more serious than adultery. (Alma 39:5.)

The Savior, in the Sermon on the Mount, indicated that looking on other persons with lust is to commit adultery with them in the heart, and certainly the current tendency to "pet" comes well within that definition.

The Savior said something about this matter in modern revelation which should frighten every person who has a tendency toward this sin.

In the Doctrine and Covenants, we read this:

"Many have turned away from my commandments and have not kept them.

"There were among you adulterers and adultresses; some of whom have turned away from you, and others remain with you that hereafter shall be revealed.

"Let such beware and repent speedily, lest judgment shall come upon them as a snare, and their folly shall be made manifest, and their works shall follow them in the eyes of the people.

"And verily I say unto you, as I have said before, he that looketh on a woman to lust after her, or if any shall commit adultery in their hearts, they shall not have the Spirit but shall deny the faith *and shall fear*.

"Wherefore, I, the Lord, have said that the fearful, and the unbelieving, and all liars, and whosoever loveth and maketh a lie, and the whoremonger, and the sorcerer, shall have their part in that lake which burneth with fire and brimstone, *which is the second death*." (D&C 63:13-17. Italics added.)

What the Lord said on Mt. Sinai about sex abuse is still the divine law to all mankind. No amount of permissiveness can make debauchery acceptable to him.

CURE BY SURRENDER?

A dangerous and frightening philosophy is sweeping over the world as corruption becomes more widespread. It is that of surrendering to evil, living with it and accepting it, and no longer regarding it as being wrong.

For example, Great Britain is fighting its drug problem by giving in to it. The largest supplier of heroin and other heavy drugs in that country is now the government itself.

Deciding that it cannot fight the drug evil by opposing it, Britain now accepts it as a fact of life and, under direction of Parliament itself, authorizes doctors to write prescriptions for drug addicts, and to supply the drugs, often as free gifts from the government.

America is doing essentially the same things with immorality. Legislature after state legislature is now legalizing prostitution, even lowering to sixteen the age at which a child may enter this dastardly business.

These same legislatures are legalizing homosexuality, a thing for which the Lord anciently prescribed capital punishment.

Some women's clubs, instead of fighting prostitution as good women should, are now suggesting that definitely defined red-light districts be re-established as a means of getting the crimson women off the streets. They say, "Accept the fact that there is a demand for prostitution, and provide for it."

Failing to see the evil in pornography, at least one church group is now putting the worst kind of adulterous acts on movies as a part of "religious" instruction — if you can believe it — as a means of giving what they call sex education to their young people in classes under a "religious" sponsorship!

This course of instruction, first projected near Milwaukee, would have co-educational groups between the ages of twelve and fourteen years see on the screen closeups of the human anatomy and then watch demonstrations of certain sex acts which are among the worst perversions of a wicked world.

It is no wonder that decent-minded people are seeking legal action to stop such depravity parading under the name of education.

Another phase of this overall problem is the willingness of men and women to resort to abortions to cover up their sexual excesses, literally taking unborn life in the process. This has become so extensive that in some American and European cities such operations outnumber live births. In Japan, the condition is so serious that statesmen there fear that before long they will have a nation of only old people.

The military of virtually all nations has surrendered to immorality, and instead of trying to prevent it, merely hand out prophylactics for the convenience of the men, obviously expecting that all will use them. Have they never heard of chastity?

Some schools are following suit by making the pill freely available. At some colleges, boys and girls are allowed to take the opposite sex into their dormitories overnight, the only restriction being that the visitors leave by 6:00 A.M. to avoid interference with classes. At certain schools no objection is raised when boys and girls occupy the same apartments without benefit of marriage.

The public attitude on liquor is no different. In spite of all that liquor costs in lives, suffering, broken homes and an economic loss running into the billions each year, we still make liquor more available, so that drinking, like immorality, is made an increasingly acceptable part of our way of life.

Right-thinking people must realize that public acceptance of evil does not make it good. Black cannot be made white by law nor by popularity. Sin is sin no matter where it is found, or under what circumstances.

Fads and fashion should never be allowed to blind a sensible mind to the moral traps of today. The assertion that "everyone does it" is a falsehood.

When depraved man lowers moral standards and attempts to nullify what God has said, shall we follow him?

More than ever, we must stand in holy places, and avoid all the sins of a modern Babylon, that we may protect ourselves against her plagues. The Almighty will not forever allow this depravity to continue.

OUT OF SIGHT AND MIND

There is a saying among advertising men that goes like this: "Out of sight, out of mind." The theory is that when a product is no longer advertised before the buying public, it is no longer purchased. Hence, it is said, all products require constant advertising to make them survive on the market.

This may be true of much that is offered for sale, but there is one area in which the statement does not hold true. That is in the field of pornography.

And why not? Because the devil has a way of keeping evil thoughts and experiences alive in the minds of his victims, long after the offensive thing has occurred.

A clean-minded man was once appointed to serve on a committee to fight pornography. So that all committeemen would know what they were to fight, they were asked to view some pornographic pictures.

This particular man had never seen a pornographic picture before. The samples he was shown with the committee were repulsive in the extreme. He determined to do battle against them with all his power, which he did, having a wholesome influence upon the youth among whom he labored.

But the evil pictures would not leave his own memory. Daily occurrences brought them back to mind. Constantly he fought them, and yet they continued to persist.

As he described his experience, he told of a beautiful young lady being photographed in a seductive pose, and said he could hardly believe that a pretty girl would do such a beastly thing.

He discovered that the devil never ceases his temptations. The man's memory itself became a corrupting thing, and the devil used that memory as a means of trying to break down his resistance. Fortunately the man was stronger than the devil, and although he regretted the constant and unwelcome recollection of the evil pictures, he was strong enough to control himself.

But what do such pictures do to weaker people? What about young folks in whom the sex drives are just beginning to form? What would memories of seeing such pictures do to them when they are dating? Would the impulse arise to do the same things that were done by the people in the pictures?

The memory of evil sights persist in young people's minds even more forcefully than they did in the mind of the strong man on the anti-pornography committee.

Then what is the answer? It is simple: Don't look at such things. Don't buy them. If you have them in your possession, do not show them to anyone else. Destroy them.

Evil lives on in the memory, sometimes more persistently than does good. The devil sees to that. He knows that sex temptation is one of the strongest he has, and he never hesitates to use it.

Parents and young people alike — those who love righteousness — must learn never to put evil into their minds; never to allow pornography in movies, still pictures or otherwise, to become a part of their memories.

President McKay used to teach: "First a thought, then an act." It is true. Hence we must forever keep our thoughts clean, and prevention is the best way of doing so. Abstinence from all evil is our best protection.

IS "PORNO" A DISEASE?

Modern diagnosticians have a tendency to look on certain behavior patterns as diseases.

The steady drinker who has become an alcoholic is now said to suffer from a disease. Obscenity with its related menace of pornography is now being called a disease. Some say a craving for pornography is itself a disease. What is a disease anyway?

Webster's dictionary gives at least two definitions worth considering. One is "a condition of ill health or malfunction of a living organism." Another is a broader one and says, "any disordered or unwholesome condition." If we use the word as a verb, we have "to derange or make unhealthy."

It requires a certain mental condition to crave pornography and obscenity. Is it to be a disease of the mind? If we used the definition of the verb, we can certainly agree that pornography can "make unhealthy" the minds of those who indulge in it.

Maybe such people are sick. Maybe we have a national "disease" on our hands and if so, shouldn't we regard a craving for filth as a disease and fight it as we would fight polio or smallpox?

At a recent meeting of the Commission on Obscenity and Pornography at Los Angeles, Milton S. Gelman, chairman, expressed himself as follows: "Pornography and obscenity proliferation represent the symptoms of the disease and not the disease itself." The disease, he explained, is the decline of the social and physical standards of a community that permits "dirty bookstores" and "love parlors" to penetrate communities.

Decent citizens must keep their values straight. It is all too easy to excuse wrongdoing by saying the person involved is suffering from a disease. Bank robbery is not a disease. Rape is not a disease. Highway speeding is not a disease, and neither is drunkenness nor is indulgence in obscenity.

A person does not exercise his free agency in whether or not he catches cold or pneumonia, but he does exercise his agency in whether he robs or rapes or speeds or drinks or goes to X-rated movies.

That is where the difference lies. That is why immorality is not a disease and why it is plain unvarnished sin. We need not repent of pneumonia or appendicitis, but most certainly we must repent of sin.

Let us not sedate ourselves by trying to class sin as a disease. Let us recognize obscenity and its child, pornography, for what they are and fight them as depravities for which the only real cure is repentance.

A MORAL PRINCIPLE

"Religious dogmatic tyranny versus the liberated woman is the latest debate in the continuing freedom-of-choice battle."

This was the opening sentence of a recent discussion on abortion which was carried in a widely circulated magazine, written by a well-known woman columnist. The article attempted to show that every woman should have the full control of her own body without restrictions from church or state, and that political pressures should not be imposed upon her.

How far afield some people will go to justify their selfish desires as well as their political motives! Who can believe that abortion is a political issue? Of course some attempt to make it so, and endeavor to use political means to achieve their purposes. Basically, abortion is a moral and religious matter. And who makes it so? The Almighty himself! It is in the word of God, given in the revelations to men — and women!

It is an offense against God to destroy life — even embryonic life — except as the Lord himself sets down the conditions. He has imposed capital punishment for serious sins, whether opponents of the idea like it or not. And he has said through his servants that where a mother's life is endangered because of most unusual conditions, medical action may be taken.

The entire thrust of the gospel is for the preservation and exaltation of life. Every one of us should remember why we are on earth, why we are passing through mortality. Worldly people who know not of the gospel may believe — if they wish — that the earth came about by some stellar accident, that life developed spontaneously, and that we evolved from microscopic forms which eventually became human. Latter-day Saints, however, do not need to believe such speculation. They know by revelation that God created this earth. They know that he created it for us, who are his spirit children who lived with him in an eternity prior to the formation of this world.

They likewise know that we are here as a part of a divine plan of salvation which gives us the opportunity to develop into that kind of perfection which is like unto God.

They also know that God provided family life and reproduction of the species here as a means of bringing his spirit children into the world, that they might have this mortal experience.

People who have this knowledge could not sensibly reject the idea of proper marriage or proper family life. People who understand the gospel could not in good conscience refuse to have children, nor would they destroy an unwelcome fetus.

Proper motherhood is a divine institution — the highest opportunity of womanhood. Can there be anything enslaving about it, then, that women must be liberated from it? What right-thinking woman would seek liberation from God and his ways? When God commands, there is certainly no religious tyranny involved, as the woman writer indicates.

To "liberate" ourselves from the laws of God is a form of apostasy, is it not?

THE SANCTITY OF LIFE

"Abortion must be considered one of the most revolting and sinful practices of our time." This is the repeated warning to Latter-day Saints as issued by the First Presidency of the Church.

As abortion becomes ever more popular among the people of the world, and even among some of our own people, it is well to remember what the prophets of God have said:

"Abortion must be considered one of the most revolting and sinful practices of our time. . . .

"Members of the Church guilty of being parties to the sin of abortion must be subjected to the disciplinary action of the councils of the Church as circumstances warrant," the Presidency continued.

They urged members to "neither submit to nor perform an abortion except in the rare cases where it is medically necessary." And even then, "it should be done only after counseling with the local presiding priesthood authority and after receiving divine confirmation through prayer."

Elder James E. Faust, in discussing this question before a general conference of the Church, among other things said:

"One of the most evil myths of our day is that a woman who has joined hands with God in creation can destroy that creation because she claims the right to control her own body. Since the life within her is not her own, how can she justify its termination and deflect that life from an earth which it may never inherit?"

Elder Faust continued:

"For the unborn, only two possibilities are opened: It can become a live human being, or a dead, unborn child."

Elder Faust further said:

"Since becoming a parent is such a transcending blessing and since each child is so precious and brings so much happiness, a cardinal purpose of marriage and of life itself is to bring forth new life within this partnership with God.

"Obligations inherent in the creation of precious human life are a sacred trust which, if faithfully kept, will keep us from degenerating into moral bankrupts and from becoming mere addicts of lust."

He then continued:

"Experts tell us that the necessity of terminating unborn life is rarely justified for purely medical or psychiatric reasons.

"Some justify abortions because the unborn may have been exposed to drugs or disease or may have birth defects. Where in all the world is the physically or mentally perfect man or woman?

"Is life not worth living unless it is free from handicaps? Experience in working with handicapped children would suggest that human nature frequently rises above its impediments and that in Shakespeare's words, 'They say best men are molded out of faults.'

"It is the belief of those who are members of this Church that human life is so hallowed and precious that there is an accountability to God on the part of those who invoke the sacred fountains of life."

With such warnings as these from the leaders of the Church, can any Latter-day Saint submit to an unnecessary abortion?

THE SILENT MAJORITY

The "silent majority" expression has related to many subjects. More recently it has seen expression in the restriction of smoking in airplanes and other public places, and this is certainly good.

But should not this majority begin to become vocal with respect to spending public monies by the millions to provide free abortions to women who don't want their pregnancies completed?

In 1975 the Associated Press carried an announcement by the U.S. Department of Health, Education and Welfare, that fifty million dollars of tax money are being spent every year to provide free abortions to "poor women."

It may be presumed that all women who submit to unnecessary abortions are "poor women" or "poor creatures" or "poor, misguided souls" but that is not the connotation the HEW officials have in mind. They speak of women who do not have the price to pay for these hazardous operations.

Dr. Louis M. Hellman, assistant secretary of the department for "population affairs," admitted to the Associated Press that his department provides about 275,000 abortions to women on welfare at the average cost to the USA of $180 each.

And then, astonishingly, he said that he regards this as a "good bargain" because he indicates that if the women had carried their children full term the cost to taxpayers would have been $2,200 each.

"A bargain" he calls it. Life destruction at a bargain! A saving of $2,000 per woman. A great bargain!

Can anyone estimate the value of a single life? What if another Edison or a Lindbergh or a Lincoln or a Washington was wiped out and prohibited from coming into mortal life by these wretched operations? What if a Peter or a Paul or a John the Revelator had been the fetus which was destroyed? Or what if *any* son or daughter of God had been thus deprived? Are we to measure the life of a child against $2,000? Where is our sense of values? Where is our sense of decency?

It is interesting that in the same newspaper another article quotes Bernard N. Nathanson, M.D., once a prime advocate of abortions, but now beginning to repent. Dr. Nathanson headed a clinic in New York which alone destroyed the fetuses of sixty thousand infants in eighteen months. Now they rise to haunt him.

Says the doctor, "There is no longer a serious doubt in my mind that human life exists within the womb from the very onset of pregnancy." He referred to heart and brain responses in human embryos. He says that to deny that abortion is an interruption of a process producing a citizen of the world is the "crassest kind of moral evasiveness."

Writing in a recent issue of the *New England Journal of Medicine,* the learned doctor says that we must now look to the "moral climate" of the nation, and "reclaim the primacy of the family in our society." Thank Heaven!

In New York, abortion "mills" operate, and doctors have been paid at the rate of $40 per hour to do the filthy work. They too were paid tax money.

If the "silent majority" knew all the facts of abortion they would rise up, silent no longer, and fight the condition. Are they not taxpayers — and Christians?

THAT UNBORN LIFE

Life is life, and when we purposely end its existence we destroy something that we have no power to replace. Such life may be in its embryonic state, but it is life nevertheless. Such life has the full potential for ultimate development, and in the case of the human embryo it might become another Lincoln, another Shakespeare, another Einstein, or another very good next-door neighbor. Who knows?

God provided life, and he made it in various forms. All life is the work of his hands. But human life is different in that it provides mortal existence for the children of God who are spirits fathered by him, spirits for whom we are to provide earthly tabernacles.

Mortality is essential for the spirit children of God. It is part of the way to perfection. It is through mortality and only through it that their eternal development can come.

We had a preexistence. We now have mortal life wherein we obtain flesh-and-bone bodies as tabernacles for our spirits. Without those bodies there can be no eternal life in the sense of our ultimately becoming like God.

Could a child of God, for example, have a resurrection if it never had a body? And yet resurrection is essential to our eternal life. Could it be tried and tested in mortal experience as God designs, if it were not given the opportunity of even entering mortality? Without mortality there is no immortality in the sense of eternal life and exaltation.

If we prevent a spirit from entering mortality — if we destroy even the embryo of mortal life so that it cannot be born — what do we do to that spirit and its eternal advancement? Do we have the right to impose such an affliction upon it?

Why do we suppose God commanded us to multiply and replenish the earth? Not for the sake of the earth, certainly, for the earth was made for us. It was to give his spirit offspring the opportunity of obtaining bodies so that that door would be opened to them for the enjoyment of eternal life and exaltation in his presence.

Can we lay any claim whatever to an understanding of the gospel if we deliberately set out to frustrate the purposes of God by preventing birth?

ON LIMITING FAMILIES

Our present-day leaders of the Church have been wonderfully outspoken in teaching the people that marriage is sacred, and that it is for the rearing of good families within the faith.

Former presidents of the Church have likewise been forthright in their instruction on this point.

President Brigham Young said:

"There are multitudes of pure and holy spirits waiting to take tabernacles. Now what is our duty? To prepare tabernacles for them: to take a course that will not tend to drive those spirits into the families of the wicked, where they will be trained in wickedness, debauchery, and every species of crime. It is the duty of every righteous man and woman to prepare tabernacles for all the spirits they can. . . .

"To check the increase of our race has its advocates among the influential and powerful circles of society in our nation and in other nations. The same practice existed forty-five years ago, and various devices were used by married persons to prevent the expenses and responsibilities of a family of children, which they must have incurred had they suffered nature's laws to rule pre-eminent.

"That which was practiced then in fear and against reproving conscience is now boldly trumpeted abroad as one of the best means of ameliorating the miseries and sorrows of humanity.

"The wife of the servant man is the mother of eight or ten healthy children, while the wife of the master is the mother of one or two poor, sickly children, devoid of vitality and constitution, and of daughters, unfit, in their turn, to be mothers, and the health and vitality which nature has denied them through the irregularities of their parents are not repaired in the least by their education." *(Discourses of Brigham Young.)*

President Wilford Woodruff declared:

"Another word of the Lord to me is that it is the duty of these young men here in the land of Zion to take the daughters of Zion to wife, and prepare tabernacles for the spirits of men, which are the children of our Father in heaven. They are waiting for tabernacles, they are ordained to come here, and they ought to be born in the land of Zion instead of Babylon."

On the same subject President Joseph F. Smith said:

"While man was yet immortal, before sin had entered the world, our Heavenly Father himself performed the first marriage. He united our first parents in the bonds of holy matrimony and commanded them to be fruitful and to multiply and replenish the earth. This command has never been changed, abrogated or annulled; but it has continued in force throughout all the generations of mankind." (*Juvenile Instructor,* Vol. 37, p. 400, July 1, 1902.)

Joseph F. Smith also said:

"I regret, I think it is a crying evil, that there should exist a sentiment or a feeling among any members of the Church to curtail the birth of their children. I think that is a crime wherever it occurs, where husband and wife are in possession of health and vigor and are free from impurities that would be entailed upon their posterity.

"I believe that where people undertake to curtail or prevent the birth of their children that they are going to reap disappointment by and by.

"I have no hesitancy in saying that I believe that this is one of the greatest crimes of the world today, this evil practice." (*Gospel Doctrine,* pp. 278-279.)

Can Latter-day Saints expect any clearer statement pertaining to this much-debated question? Need any go astray?

ANOTHER WARNING

From time to time medical research reveals further risks in the use of contraceptive pills. The U.S. Food and Drug Administration has issued repeated cautions to women who indulge.

Private physicians likewise have issued warnings to their own patients on the subject. Following is another statement from government sources:

"WASHINGTON (UPI) — The Food and Drug Administration plans to tell women over forty to avoid birth control pills.

"The FDA said Thursday it has drafted warning labels for birth control pills which will inform users that sex hormones in the pill can cause birth defects such as stunted limbs and malformed hearts.

"About ten million women in America use the pills. The new warnings . . . will tell women who take them they face an increased risk of suffering fatal and nonfatal heart attacks.

"Women who wish to stop taking the pill and become pregnant will be advised to wait at least three months because "studies show there is a possible increased risk of spontaneous abortion in women who become pregnant shortly after discontinuing the pill."

Sad as these health problems may be, probably the worst phase of "pill addiction" comes in the use of this contraceptive among hosts of young women and girls, many still in high school, mostly unmarried, who have become promiscuous.

Some have felt "safe" in using the pill, forgetting that the moral implication is far more important than the pretended "safety" they may experience.

No one can gainsay the fact that the pill has contributed immeasurably to promiscuity worldwide. With it has come a wave of venereal disease which authorities say now exceeds the epidemic stage. It has become a plague.

A Seattle dispatch, carried also by UPI, indicates that now little girls, nine, ten and eleven years of age, are asking for birth control devices. "Dr. Gerry Oliva, a pediatrician at Children's Hospital in Oakland, Calif., and a medical director for Planned Parenthood in San Francisco and Alameda counties, said in Seattle:

'A lot of them are brought in by their parents. But many of them just find their way to us. The word is out in the community and we're seeing girls from all over.

'Right now it's a small number — less than 5 percent — but the problem is the young girls coming to us in ever increasing numbers. A lot of them we don't see for contraception, we see in the high-risk pregnancy program. We see kids eleven and twelve delivering babies, so we're not getting to them early enough.' "

Werner Fornos, who runs the nation's first high school birth control clinic in Washington, D. C., is quoted by UPI as saying that one in every three pregnancies in the United States involves a teenager. He said:

"We had 750,000 teenage pregnancies in the United States in 1974 and that should make us realize we have a new epidemic we can't afford to tolerate in this country."

Can we fail to see what immorality is doing to us? Have we not the courage to stem this tide? Only chastity can do it. Our very survival as a race will ultimately depend upon our attitude toward virtue.

6.

HONESTY

AND

INTEGRITY

CHRISTIANITY AND HONESTY

The true Christian religion cannot be separated from true Christian living. If we do not obey the Savior and keep his commandments, can we in all truthfulness call ourselves Christians? We may take his name upon us, but if we fail to follow in his footsteps, our acts belie our professions, and we become hypocritical.

One of the worst afflictions in modern Christianity is that of dishonesty. High professions are made by many, but too often the performance is not what the Lord would expect.

Can there really be any Christian living without honesty?

When we think of what dishonesty does to us, it is incredible that any true Christian would submit to it. It leads to lying and to crime, to deception, theft, infidelity, and to immorality — in fact, where does it end?

It would be difficult indeed to have a living faith in Christ without doing his works. To profess belief in him and yet refuse to live his laws is a dishonest act in itself. Is it not true that dishonesty is a form of apostasy from Christ?

When the Savior told us to love our neighbors as ourselves, surely he spoke of honesty. One cannot do unto others as we would be done by if we have impure motives. When he advised reconciliation with those we have offended, or by whom we have been offended, surely he included honesty as a part of the consideration. Could there be any reconciliation without honesty, sincerity, and an earnest desire to do the right thing?

No one in all scripture received the stern rebukes from the Savior that he leveled at the hypocrites. And why? Because of their basic dishonesty, their desire to sail under false colors, their determination to be wolves in sheep's clothing.

The Lord hates a lie, and denounces it most vigorously. It is bad enough to lie under stress, as some do, but to live a lie — and make it a practice — is intolerable. And yet, how many Christians do that very thing?

If an honest man is the noblest work of God, in what category do the dishonest place themselves?

A WAY OF LIFE – REALLY?

Yes, really. Lying is becoming a way of life for large masses of people. So is cheating.

Readers of the *National Observer* were shocked by a large headline carried on its front page. It read: "To lie is a verb — and also a lifestyle." The editorial asked: "Has society delivered honesty a knock-out blow? Do we care about it any more? Does it matter?"

Lying and cheating go hand in hand. Dishonest persons do both. But God denounces them. He regards dishonesty as one of the unclean things which no true Christian should tolerate.

Each of us may easily measure the degree of our own honesty. Let us ask ourselves a few simple questions:

Do we think "white lies" are acceptable?

Do we lie to avoid embarrassment?

Do we practice deception in any degree?

Do we pay our bills — all of them?

Are we any more honest with God than we are with our fellowmen?

Do we steal?

Do we coerce?

Do we engage in shoplifting?

Do we cheat doctors and dentists by receiving of their service and never paying them what we owe?

Do we cheat our grocers, our newsboys, our landlords, or other people with whom we do business?

Dishonesty in all its forms is reprehensible. How can a person claim to be a Christian and be deceptive, or refuse to pay his bills, or steal, or cheat?

Only the Christlike may go with Christ.

THE NEED OF BUSINESS

A prominent minister in an eastern city submitted to twenty employers of large numbers of workmen this question: "What is the greatest need of the business world today?"

Each of the twenty gave the same answer: "Personal honesty."

The reason? Thievery by employes is one of the main problems of business today. It has reached such proportions that in some instances business houses have declared bankruptcy and quit.

Public thievery, added to thefts by employes, runs into the billions of dollars each year. Watch dogs, plain-clothes men, uniformed officers, and electric detection devices all have been used to stop this plague, but it goes on — a terrible and frightening testimonial to the loss of character on the part of millions of people.

Most of the thieves who are caught in either shoplifting or employe thefts are admittedly Christians who claim to believe in God, and who go to church on Sunday as an expression of their faith.

But what good is their faith when their works are diametrically opposed to the principles of their religion? Have they never learned that faith without works is dead? Have they never heard of hypocrisy and the manner in which the Lord denounced it?

Thieves! Thieves! Thieves! Can they ever expect salvation? Can repentance come to them? Are they able to reconstruct their lives and overcome this detestable trait in their characters? Are they able to make restitution to those from whom they have stolen?

Much is said about crime in its broader sense. But isn't shoplifting a crime? Isn't it a crime for an employe to take property that belongs to his employer?

Elder Albert E. Bowen of the Council of the Twelve once discussed thievery in these terms:

"Why does one steal? Obviously to get what one desires and might otherwise have to do without. Stealing has its inception in covetousness. If men did not covet they would not steal. The thief is indifferent to the suffering of others. Altogether he presents a sorry sample of qualities. He is covetous, lacking in self-control, indifferent, cruel.

"Basically, honesty is a matter of character. Honesty and the highest ideals of manhood are bound up inseparably together.

"But harmful as thieving may be to the victim, it is vastly more devastating to the perpetrator of the theft.

"He robs himself of his own self-respect, which is one of the most nearly irreparable losses anyone may sustain. A man may lose the esteem of his fellows and survive the loss if supported by the consciousness of his own rectitude. It is not so important what others think of him but what he knows about himself is of transcendent importance.

"The thief practices, of necessity, the art of deceit and becomes, in consequence, devious in his ways. His mental processes are sinuous. He does not trust and is not trusted.

"Even though he has not been found out and moves freely in society, he knows himself to be something other than what people take him to be. To that extent he knows that he is an impostor and a fraud.

"Observance of the eighth commandment, on the other hand, never brings remorse. Instead of begetting fear it inspires confidence and courage. It preserves self-respect, encourages forthrightness and discounts deceit.

"Like all God's commandments it takes cognizance of the conditions necessary to a man's peace and happiness, and admonishes him in the way of life that brings their realization."

DISHONESTY IS FATAL

Dishonesty raises its head in the most unexpected places. For years we have known about it in student cheating, in shoplifting indulged in largely by mothers and children, and in deceptions even among the pious.

Now comes the disclosure, as indicated in a recent edition of the *U.S. News & World Report,* that fraud in the Alaskan pipeline project already has reached the billion-dollar mark, with the job as yet only half completed.

With that also comes the recent discovery that dishonesty has been rampant in our sale of grain to foreign nations. New Orleans is the chief shipping point for such transactions. News reports indicate that millions of dollars worth of grain has been stolen there, involving some men who were hired to prevent such crimes.

Disclosure of bribes among lawmakers and elected officials are shocking to a citizenry that expects integrity on the part of its public servants.

It seems almost as though dishonesty is becoming a way of life. It reminds one of the Gadianton robber days of the Book of Mormon, when nothing was safe from corruption. Are we reaching that point today?

Dishonesty can destroy us. It spelled the doom of the Nephites. It undermined ancient Greece and Rome. And it can spell the end of modern nations if not checked.

The Savior faced the dishonest of his day and called them hypocrites. Is that not a good name for the dishonest of today? Are not deceptive ones wolves in sheep's clothing, pretending to be what they are not, and for predatory reasons?

In dishonesty, as in alcoholism, reformation must begin with the individual. Each of us must determine that we shall not become involved in it.

For Latter-day Saints there can be only one standard of conduct, and that is well expressed in our Article of Faith which says: "We believe in being honest. . . ."

HONEST WORK, HONEST PAY

Most of the ills of the world can be traced to dishonesty in some form or another. Selfishness breeds dishonesty, and dishonesty in turn multiplies selfishness. How much better the world would be if both could be abolished!

In these days when so many people take advantage of others, the question of labor and pay for that labor is uppermost in the thoughts of most people in business.

Workers frequently claim they are not adequately paid for their labor. Employers often say that they are not getting the proper labor for the wages they pay.

Certain it is that there is room for improvement on both sides. There is no place for shoddy work on the part of an employe; no place for carelessness; no place for deception. Neither is there place for anything approaching dishonesty on the part of an employer, too many of whom do take advantage of employes.

There is one sure answer to all disputes arising between employer and employe, and that is observance of the Golden Rule. Is there any reason why it should not apply to business?

If every employe were honest enough to do to his employer as he himself would be done by; if every employer were forthright enough to do to his employes as he himself would be done by, all labor troubles would disappear.

Everyone would be the richer for it, frayed nerves would be a thing of the past; conflicts, which sometimes cost life and limb, would completely disappear.

There is such a condition as business harmony and it can be reached through an honest application of that great rule of the Savior, set down in the Sermon on the Mount.

As Christians, can we honestly do less?

GOOD CHECKS AND BAD

A service station prominently displayed this sign: "Only Approved Checks Accepted."

Another station announced: "No Checks Accepted."

A grocery store told its customers in a prominent sign at the checkstand: "Only approved checks accepted for amount of purchase."

These signs represent a cross section of many more in almost every type of business in almost every city and town. Why? Because so many bad checks are written that merchants can no longer take chances on being defrauded.

What a commentary on the honesty — or lack of it — among the American people! How long does anyone suppose a society can go on without sufficient character to sustain basic honesty?

Thievery, dishonesty, deception, covetousness — all are severely condemned by the Lord. Can Christians suppose that God will admit any dishonest person into his kingdom? Or don't they have enough faith to make them worry about his kingdom?

Our Christian society is built upon integrity. Without it, our way of life will collapse. If we allow dishonesty to weave itself deeply into the fabric of our lives, we invite moral suicide.

When we say in our Articles of Faith that "we believe in being honest," we express one of the most important tenets of our religion. Honesty is as basic to true Christianity as baptism or the resurrection. It is the foundation of all character development.

Just as no man can see the kingdom of heaven without baptism, so no dishonest person will see it either unless he sincerely repents.

Isn't it amazing that one hotel in New York, in a single year, lost 18,000 towels, 355 silver coffee pots, 15,000 finger bowls and a hundred Bibles?

Some insurance companies say that they believe 75 percent of all claims submitted to them are dishonest in overstating the loss.

Two kinds of thievery are most common. One is shoplifting, indulged in sometimes by the "best" people, and the other is writing bad checks, principally passed at grocery stores.

To resort to dishonesty is to apostatize to that extent from the Christian way of life. Apostasy from Christ becomes anti-Christ, and to adopt that is to put God out of our lives.

PUBLIC HONESTY

Assaults on honesty in public office have shaken the nation again in recent months and the end is not yet. What may come in months and years ahead no one can tell, but this type of experience makes us aware as seldom before of the necessity of maintaining integrity in both public and private life.

Elder Albert E. Bowen, a member of the Council of the Twelve from 1937 to 1953, and an astute public servant and a humble apostle of the Lord, spoke out in firm language on this subject. It is so pertinent today that we reproduce below what he said:

"Honesty embraces truth and requires fidelity to principle. In this realm lies what we might designate as honesty in public life. It requires that men in public office should not graft even within the law.

"Fidelity here often calls for a high order of moral courage. One hears of legislators in state and nation who talk one way and vote another.

"Among friends and in confidence they condemn policies and the laws projected to effectuate them, yet officially they vote the passage of those laws merely because they fear the course of right as they see it might not be popular and to follow it might terminate their official careers.

"They would rather violate their consciences than lose the glamor and power of official position. Such men constitute a far greater menace to our country's safety than do all the propagandists of alien philosophies put together.

"We need fear no invasion from without so long as we are sound to the core within.

"Every act of our lives, every concept of our intellects, every yearning of our souls, to be worthy must be impregnated with the quality of honesty — that quality which gives integrity to the internal structure of a man and fits him for every trust."

IMMORALITY IN HIGH PLACES

The disclosure of wrongdoing and questionable activities by officials in this nation's capital brought a strong statement by President Spencer W. Kimball condemning an attitude of "indifference toward serious acts of wrong-doing" among public servants throughout the nation.

The Church president described as "shocking" the disclosures and charges concerning questionable activities of officials in Washington.

Although President Kimball's statement concerned only those officials in the United States, it was noted that this country isn't alone as far as such activities are concerned among public servants. Dishonest and immoral practices go on in almost every other country of the world among government officials and public servants.

President Kimball called upon all elected and appointed officials to observe the "high moral principles which have contributed to this nation's greatness."

In a strong statement issued from his office in Salt Lake City, President Kimball said:

"New disclosures and charges regarding questionable activities of public servants in Washington, D.C., in addition to those in recent months and years, are shocking indeed.

"It is time for both elected and appointed officials, regardless of party, in our government nationally and locally to appraise themselves and their practices. There appears to be too often an attitude of indifference toward serious acts of wrongdoing.

"There is no better time than now, in this bicentennial year of our nation's birth, for a rededication to the high moral principles which have contributed to this nation's greatness.

"The workings of our government should be an example to the world — in uncompromising integrity, in wise and prudent stewardship of public funds, in personal morality, including fidelity in marriage, and in an openness on activities which will build the confidence of the electorate. The citizenry should expect no less.

"We remind public servants of a slogan of President Grover Cleveland: 'Public office is a public trust.'

"And also of President Theodore Roosevelt's statement: 'It is better to be faithful than famous.' This nation can be no stronger than its families.

"America cannot remain strong by ignoring the commandments of the Lord given to Moses on Sinai.

"It is time our government officials and all of us reaffirm our motto: 'In God We Trust,' and conduct our lives accordingly."

GAMES OF CHANCE

Something for nothing! That is the pot of gold that many seek at the end of the rainbow. And it is just as nebulous as the rainbow itself.

Gambling, whether in the form of slot machines, card tables or raffles, lotteries or betting on dog and horse races, becomes more and more popular in worldly circles. Resort towns have been made rich on gambling. Millionaires build larger hotels and more dazzling casinos, all from gambling. But does this make gambling good?

Christian people should look carefully to the moral side of gambling.

If games of chance are good, why do strong governments and sound states of the Union legislate against them? If they are good, why does our Church oppose them?

In the days of President Joseph F. Smith, some argued that lotteries were acceptable providing the objective for which the money was raised was good. So some tried to conduct lotteries — believe it or not — to finance missionary work! And what did the First Presidency say about that?

We quote from President Smith: "Is it proper to raffle property for the benefit of missionaries? No! Raffling is a game of chance and hence leads to gambling. For that reason if for no other, it should not be encouraged by the young men of the Church. . . .

"Among the vices of the present age, gambling is very generally condemned. Devices for raising money by appealing to the gambling instinct are common accessories at socials, fairs, and the like.

"Whatever may be the condition elsewhere, this custom is not to be sanctioned within the Church and any organization allowing such is in opposition to the counsel and instruction of the General Authorities of the Church." (*Gospel Doctrine*, pp. 326-327.)

President Brigham Young taught that raffling is gambling and that if parents raffle, the children will gamble.

The handbook of instruction to the leaders of the Church reads: "Raffling and games of chance are highly objectionable and must not be sponsored or permitted in connection with any church function. The selling of chances in any form, however disguised, is not to be permitted."

As in most other things, older people set a pattern for the youth. If mature people teach their youth gambling and other evils, what may we expect of the next generation?

COST OF GAMBLING

For years the Church has advised its people against all forms of gambling. Each of the presidents has spoken out against it. And the advice has been good. How good?

Recently the *U.S. News & World Report* ran a list of principal forms of crime in America, with the cost per year of each. Losses in gambling led all the rest.

Gambling losses were five times the narcotics bill; more than twenty times the cost of hijacking; four times the losses in embezzlements, fraud and forgery combined; ten times greater than robbery, burglary, theft and shoplifting; twenty-five times greater than vandalism and arson, and more than twice the cost of maintaining all federal, state and local police, plus the expense of operating our penal system and the courts which handle criminals.

And what was the cost of gambling? Thirty billion dollars — *per year*.

And yet, some states are introducing lotteries as a means of increasing their income. Some clubs — even some religious groups — sponsor gambling games.

With the thirty billion dollars lost in gambling, think of the constructive things that could be done if the money were diverted into worthwhile lines! What would thirty billion dollars a year do to help the starving peoples overseas? What if it were used to pay off the national debt! What if that amount of money were spent each year to reduce taxes in our communities, where because of shortage of funds essential services must be curtailed!

Is there anything good to be said of gambling?

WORK NOT IN DARKNESS

One of the things the Lord warned frequently about in the Book of Mormon was the work of "secret combinations." Among the Nephites those secret combinations were always destructive. They were invariably associated with crime, apostate groups, or other activities directly aligned with the evil one.

The Gadianton robbers used secrets which were handed down from Cain. Men like Korihor and other apostate teachers dealt in "works of darkness" as they led people astray, professing to have had "special" revelations urging them to do so.

There are those today who also claim such revelations. They also work in the shadow of secrecy. They hold secret meetings. They hide their true identity, going only by their first names and holding in secret their last names.

Many resort to lies and subterfuge. They teach their children to misrepresent facts. Certain among them have what they call "plural wives" and usually teach those women to pose as their "sisters" or "aunts" or simply as neighbors, and give no explanation for the large number of children in any one home.

They are masters in "cover up," yet they profess to teach a secret truth made known to them specially by some hidden process. And surprisingly enough, there are still gullible individuals who believe them.

When will people learn that "the Lord worketh not in darkness" (2 Nephi 26:23), and that he gives no secret revelations and authorizes no secret ordinations? The Lord's work is done openly and aboveboard, with the vote and voice of the congregations of the Saints. (D&C 20:63-67; 26:2.)

When devious persons come with "hush-hush" doctrines, their very secrecy should be ample warning to the faithful who must realize that the Lord "worketh not in darkness." By their devious methods such teachers brand themselves for what they are.

AS WE METE TO OTHERS

The Lord condemns dishonesty. He has said so many times.

Dishonesty, like other kinds of vice, takes many forms. Thievery is one of its names; deception is another. It provides lies in wholesale lots, as it does cheating and violation of the law. One of its most reprehensible forms is found in character assassination wherein evil people, by cowardly and lying gossip, destroy the good names of innocent ones.

Such slanderous action of course has its root in hate, and what is more ugly than hate? It is an expression of the devil himself, who is the author of hate and has taught his followers hatred from the preexistent council in heaven to the present day.

Hatred in an evil mind gives birth to damaging falsehoods that can cause irreparable harm. One of the difficulties about this is that it also gives rise to gossip by which evil things are spread about as choice morsels of conversation.

Sometimes innocent people are trapped into repeating rumors and untruths and thus they become parties to the whole malicious business, allies of evil and depraved persons.

It is no wonder that the Lord placed prominently in scripture:

"These six things doth the Lord hate: yea, seven are an abomination unto him:

"A proud look, a lying tongue, and hands that shed innocent blood,

"An heart that deviseth wicked imaginations, feet that be swift in running to mischief,

"A false witness that speaketh lies, and he that soweth discord among brethren." (Proverbs 6:16-19.)

Who has a right to blacken another's name?

Who is privileged to judge his fellowmen?

Who can righteously sit in the scorner's seat?

Who is willing to be the modern Pharisee and shout to the world, "I thank thee that I am not as other men — as this publican or this next-door neighbor or as this in-law relative of mine"?

Then why do we assume the right to gossip and condemn?

Will we not remember that in the final judgment the Lord will mete out to us as we have meted to our fellows here on earth? Even a farmer once said, "The chickens will always come home to roost."

7.

KNOWLEDGE
AND
WISDOM

HOW SHALL WE CHOOSE?

What is the difference between research and revelation? Must we choose one or the other, or may we have both?

Marvelous things have been accomplished through scientific research. This great work has given us all of our modern comforts and conveniences.

We have artificial light and central heat because of research; we likewise scan the heavens, visit the moon, send missiles to distant planets; we have eliminated plagues and epidemics which swept the earth in the past; we farm better, we travel faster, we see better with the devices research has provided.

Through a practical application of proven principles we yet shall move on to still higher standards of living, better methods in business, more effective education, and improved health.

All of these are blessings of the Lord who inspires our inventors and our scientists in many ways. That is one form of inspiration by which the Light of Christ comes to every man.

But there is another necessary source of progress, and that is direct revelation. At times deductions from uncompleted research are prematurely accepted as fact. Sometimes these deductions are contrary to divine revelation. When both are presented to us, which shall we choose?

Our great scientists — particularly Mormon scientists — assure us that there is no conflict between true religion and true science. Our religion teaches us that all truth comes from God, and that "if there is anything virtuous, lovely or of good report, or praiseworthy, we seek after these things."

But when research is incomplete, can we take preliminary deductions as being final? Shall we allow them to overthrow our faith in revelation?

The researchers working with incomplete deductions usually change their minds. They are honest in their search for truth, and therefore adjust as "new knowledge" becomes available.

But let us remember that revelation doesn't need to change its mind, and never does. Revelation comes from the Fountain of all truth, from the Almighty who made the universe and all within it. When he reveals truth, no adjustment is necessary, for his truth is eternal and everlasting.

FAITH AND KNOWLEDGE

Everyone deep in his heart has some degree of faith in God. Even some professed atheists express faith at times.

There are many who say that because they do not understand God, or cannot see him, they will not accept him. But there are many things in life that they neither see nor hear nor feel, and yet they believe in their existence.

Thomas A. Edison one time said: "We don't know what water is. We don't know what electricity is. We don't know what heat is. We have a lot of hypotheses about these things, but that is all. But we do not let our ignorance about these things deprive us of their use."

It was Robert A. Millikan, a great American scientist, who said: "I consider an intimate knowledge of the Bible an indispensable qualification of a well-educated man."

And Ralph Waldo Emerson said: "Don't be a cynic, don't waste yourself in rejection."

"God is still the best 'medicine' that we physicians can ever prescribe," said Dr. George W. Crane. "But he expects us to team up with him and utilize our wits, plus all the available drugs and other techniques that scientists have developed.

" 'God helps those who help themselves' is an adage which means that he doesn't want us lazily to ask him to do all the curing when we have other proved aids.

"But when we get out of our depth, God often steps in and produces miraculous cures, as every experienced physician can attest."

The Latter-day Saints know that God lives and they do not question him. They have great confidence in their prophets and one of the greatest testimonies of the prophets came from Joseph Smith and Sidney Rigdon when they said:

"And now, after the many testimonies which have been given of him, this is the testimony, last of all, which we give of him: That he lives!

"For we saw him, even on the right hand of God; and we heard the voice bearing record that he is the Only Begotten of the Father —

"That by him, and through him, and of him, the worlds are and were created, and the inhabitants thereof are begotten sons and daughters unto God." (D&C 76:22-24.)

TEACHING THE TRUTH

Our presiding brethren have often told us that our pulpits and classrooms are strictly for teaching gospel truths. They are not to be used as public forums in which anyone is free to proclaim his private views on gospel or other topics. Our sole object both in preaching from the pulpit and in holding classroom discussions is to convert people to the gospel of Christ.

It was the Lord who said: "And I give unto you a commandment that you shall teach one another the doctrine of the kingdom." (D&C 88:77.)

The only doctrine of the kingdom is the gospel of Christ.

Again the Lord said:

"And again, the elders, priests and teachers of this church shall teach the principles of my gospel, which are in the Bible and the Book of Mormon, in the which is the fulness of the gospel." (D&C 42:12.)

At the time this command was given (February 9, 1831), our other modern scriptures were not yet compiled.

To teach false doctrine is to lead people astray.

We should never forget what the Lord said about teachers of unsound doctrine. He warned against false prophets and false teachers. (Matthew 24:11.)   He denounced the teachings of the Pharisees (Luke 11:37-43) and said that worship through man-made doctrines is in vain. (Matthew 15:9.)

He also said this: "It were better for him that a millstone were hanged about his neck, and he cast into the sea, than that he should offend one of these little ones." (Luke 17:2.)

President Joseph Fielding Smith said, "If I ever say anything which is contrary to the scriptures, then the scriptures prevail."

It is a tendency of some individuals to expound unsound views in class discussions. This is most unfortunate. Class members who speak must know that they — like the class instructor — have the responsibility of teaching the truth and nothing but the truth.

Conversion to the gospel is our great objective in teaching and preaching. But this can never be accomplished by the use of half-truths or that which is questionable, speculative or apocryphal.

"Teach the truth" must be our constant cry. This emphasizes more than ever the need for members of the Church to be well grounded in the gospel as it is set forth in sacred scripture.

STRENGTH IN SIMPLICITY

We frequently sing a hymn in our Church meetings entitled "How Gentle God's Commands." And so all his commands are, and simple and easy to understand as well. They were that way anciently, and they are today, in spite of the efforts of some to complicate them.

As Moses said in his day: "This commandment which I command thee this day, it is not hidden from thee [the revised version says 'not too hard for thee'], neither is it far off.

"It is not in heaven, that thou shouldest say, Who shall go up for us to heaven, and bring it unto us, that we may hear it, and do it?

"Neither is it beyond the sea, that thou shouldest say, Who shall go over the sea for us, and bring it unto us, that we may hear it, and do it?

"But the word is very nigh unto thee, in thy mouth and in thy heart, that thou mayest do it." (Deuteronomy 30:11-14.)

People in those days made excuses too — anything to avoid obedience.

The commands of God are not complicated, and they are not "afar off" that we may excuse ourselves. His commands are both simple and gentle, and all who will, may understand and obey.

If the gospel was intended to be complicated, think how the Lord himself could have made it so. He was the Creator and could have talked to his listeners in terms of galaxies, trajectories, light years and higher mathematics, but he did not. Would anyone in that day have understood him? Would they have learned anything from him? He would have talked "over their heads."

Rather, he spoke in terms of putting patches on their clothing, of plowing their land and planting and harvesting their crops, and yoking together their oxen. They understood those terms, and his comparisons were meaningful to them.

Must we not follow his example in this as in other things? We must speak to be understood. We must teach in language and terms that will have meaning to our audiences. Otherwise, as Paul once said, we merely fan the air. Plainness and gentleness must always characterize our instruction. A display of learning is merely that — a display of learning — and who is impressed by it except the one who uses it?

THE SCRIPTURE SEARCH

The Savior gave us many commandments, each one a guide to help us become more like him, thus becoming eligible to enter his kingdom. In doing so, he said:

"If ye love me, keep my commandments. . . .

"He that hath my commandments, and keepeth them, he it is that loveth me: . . . If a man love me, he will keep my words: . . . He that loveth me not keepeth not my sayings." (John 14:15, 21-24.)

Though these teachings have been known to followers of Christ from the beginning, how many really believe and accept them?

One of his commandments was that we should "search the scriptures" as guides to eternal life. (John 5:39.) It is a positive command. If we truly believe in him, dare we ignore it?

Failure to read the scriptures may mean the difference between salvation and condemnation for us on the last great day. Not reading them, we cannot know what they contain, and thus we remain in ignorance of their teachings.

The Prophet Joseph taught that we cannot be saved in ignorance. Ignorance of what? Of the scriptures! Of the commandments! Of the laws of progress and salvation!

How can we obey that which we do not know? As some have said in secular life, ignorance of the law is no excuse. Neglect will not save us. We are expected to inform ourselves. Why is this? Because the gospel is actually a way of life, not a conversation piece. It is a way of life in that we are to make our lives literally conform to its pattern.

And what is the reason for this? We are the children of God. We have a destiny to become like him. We have a divine spark within us which, if encouraged, will make it possible for us actually to become Christlike — Godlike — to become perfect like our Father in Heaven.

The gospel then becomes a way of life in that it is the formula by which we can become Christlike. To become like him is to develop within ourselves those traits of character which are like his, and thus we grow into perfection.

Developing character is a matter of growth. It is like planting a seed, watering and nourishing it, and doing the things that establish routine habits that bring forth the ultimate fruit. This principle applies to both good and bad character. Seeds of sin are also planted, then nourished and developed in wrong paths, to create a criminal or a pervert.

Righteous seeds, properly planted and nourished, will produce a good soul, a righteous character.

But we must know the seeds, and carefully select them. We must intelligently plant and cultivate to achieve our goal. How can we do this in the darkness of ignorance?

To become like him, we must have *light* and *direction* and *knowledge*. This comes through the Church, through the scriptures, and through the living prophets.

Because no one can be saved in ignorance, because the glory of both man and God is intelligence, the Savior teaches us to learn of him, and to gain knowledge from the best books. The best of all books are the scriptures, so he tells us to search them, and thus learn of him; discover what his rules of perfection are, and live them.

Those rules are more than tithing, the Word of Wisdom and baptism, important as they are. They are soul-building principles which will help us to become like him. And as we become like him we assure ourselves of a place with him, not only in eternity, but in this life as well.

We cannot be saved in ignorance!

WE NEED TO KNOW

It has been said that the safety of the nation depends upon a well-informed public. The same thing may be said of the Church.

People who know their scriptures and adapt them to their daily lives are the Church members who are working out their salvation in the earth. But people who do not know the requirements of the Lord, and hence fail to obey them, are in jeopardy.

The Savior taught the Nephites to search the scriptures, even as he spoke while in Palestine. (John 5:39.) Said he to the Nephites:

"Behold, I say unto you, that ye ought to search these things. Yea, a commandment I give unto you that ye search these things diligently." (3 Nephi 23:1.)

It is dangerous to our salvation to neglect the scriptures. For example, the Lord teaches us that to be saved we must be valiant in the testimony of Jesus. If we have the testimony but do very little about it, will our testimony save us?

In section 76 of the Doctrine and Covenants we learn that such people are barred from celestial glory and are assigned to the terrestrial instead. Had they known the facts, they no doubt would have changed their ways. But ignorance will not save them. They did not read the scriptures.

We are taught that people who neglect their temple work cannot receive exaltation. (D&C 131:1-4; 132:15-18.) If they would but read what the Lord says on this subject, and become informed, they would see the risk they are taking in not attending the temple.

Ignorance of the scriptures can be our downfall. A knowledge of them will help us to meet the Lord's requirements. The Prophet Joseph told us that no one can be saved in ignorance.

If salvation means anything to us at all, we should read the scriptures and remove any ignorance on that subject which may obstruct our eternal progress. (D&C 131:6; 136:32.)

WHAT SCRIPTURES TEACH

When the apostle Peter spoke of scripture, as we read in his second epistle, he said an important thing: "Prophecy came not in old time by the will of man: but holy men of God spake as they were moved by the Holy Ghost." (2 Peter 1:21.)

This is significant. It is made especially so by this statement from modern revelation:

"And whatsoever they shall speak when moved upon by the Holy Ghost shall be scripture, shall be the will of the Lord, shall be the mind of the Lord, shall be the word of the Lord, shall be the voice of the Lord, and the power of God unto salvation." (D&C 68:4.)

Keeping this in mind will save us from many a pitfall as we learn of the hypotheses of scholars whose views are not always in harmony with holy writ.

These scriptures came from God. It is true that at times questions are raised about the Bible in its various versions because it has gone through so many uninspired hands. The miracle is that it has been preserved as well as it has. For this we must acknowledge an overruling Providence.

But modern scripture has not gone through those many hands. It has come to us in its purity and is the true word of God. It lays down for us many fundamentals which, if we would but accept, can safely guide us through the maze of philosophical speculations with which we are assailed.

A number of new books have appeared pretending to reveal the development of man from earliest times. Always they carry the flag of evolution, teaching that man evolved into human form, that then he became a hunter for his food, and later, much later, a farmer and a herdsman, and that with farming and urban life, ultimately came civilization.

"No civilization existed anywhere on the earth's surface before 3,000 B.C.," writes one distinguished scholar, who tries to imagine the development of man to a point where he discovered the use of fire, then learned to write in a crude sort of way, and still later, built great civilizations.

It is interesting, of course, to read of the discovery of libraries, irrigation systems, democratic government, architecture and art of five thousand years ago. They provide physical evidence of early man's achievements.

But they do not prove that he was once a missing link, nor that his "evolution" from lower forms of life is a proven fact. We read with interest the deductions of scholars made from discoveries by archaeologists, but whereas those discoveries are real enough, the deductions are still only deductions.

How refreshing to read what scripture says about early man, without the need to be bolstered by speculative theories. The inspired word of him who created early man, and who is the only one who really knows about early man, says this:

"The first man of all men have I called Adam. . . ." (Moses 1:34); "The first man, who is Adam. . . ." (Abraham 1:3); "Adam and Eve, who were our first parents. . . ." (1 Nephi 5:11); "Adam, who was the first man. . . ." (D&C 84:16.)

And what was Adam like — a caveman? He was intelligent and learned! His family wrote books, tilled the soil and raised crops and herds. They were taught by the Almighty himself! Could there be better? (Moses 6:5-6.)

Similar differences are noticed between the deductions of men and the scripture on other subjects. We must remember that revelation provides the truth, not speculation; fact, not fiction, and that when research is put in its proper perspective, it sustains revealed truth, for truth is never in conflict with itself. Let us accept the scripture for what it really is — the word of God.

OUR ETERNAL IDENTITY

One of the most comforting things about the gospel is our assurance of immortality, and that as part of immortality we will continue to be ourselves. We will know each other and thereby enjoy eternal life together.

This is the basis of one of our most important doctrines, that of family survival in the world to come. This is why we have temple marriage and why families are sealed together for everlasting.

What value would there be in an eternal family if members lost their identity and could not recognize each other?

President Joseph F. Smith discussed this subject with great clarity when he taught that our personal identity is both fixed and indestructible, "just as fixed and indestructible as the identity of God the Father and Jesus Christ the Son. They cannot be other than themselves." (*Gospel Doctrine,* p. 25.)

But he also gave us a further glimpse into this great doctrine, saying that as our identity is fixed in the hereafter, so it was likewise fixed during the period prior to our birth into earth life.

Since we had our origin as children of God, our identity was fixed in the preexistence even as it is preserved in the hereafter. It never has changed and never will change in the future.

Said President Smith: "We did not spring from spawn. Our spirits existed from the beginning, have existed always, and will continue forever.

"We did not pass through the ordeals of embodiment in the lesser animals in order to reach the perfection to which we have attained in manhood and womanhood, in the image and likeness of God. God was and is our Father, and his children were begotten in the flesh in his own image and likeness, male and female." (*Ibid.,* pp. 25-27.)

He then spoke of reincarnation, which was one of the false teachings circulated in his day, and said: "It is absolutely repugnant to the very soul of man to think that a civilized intelligent being might become a dog, a cow, a cat; that he might be transformed into another shape, another being. It is opposed . . . to the great truth of God that he cannot change and his children cannot change. . . . Their identity can never be changed, worlds without end. Remember that. God has revealed these principles and I know they are true."

Is it any less repugnant to suppose that we sprang from lower forms of life than to think that we might be reincarnated into them after death? Our identity does not change from one eternity to the other, it was not changed prior to our birth, and will not be changed after our death.

President Smith was a prophet of God. He spoke the words of God and taught that man was always man — the offspring of God — with the possibility sometime of becoming "perfect, even as your Father which is in heaven is perfect." (Matthew 5:48.)

Isn't it natural for children to become like their parents?

President Smith then concluded: "Our young people are diligent students. They reach out after truth and knowledge with commendable zeal, and in doing so they must necessarily adopt for temporary use many theories of men. . . . It is when these theories are settled upon as basic truth that trouble appears, and the searcher then stands in grave danger of being led hopelessly from the right way." (*Ibid.*, p. 38.)

OUR SACRED SCRIPTURE

In his great vision the first Nephi saw the manner in which the Bible was given to the gentile world. The angel who was with Nephi said, "Thou hast beheld that the book proceeded forth from the mouth of a Jew; and when it proceeded forth from the mouth of a Jew it contained the plainness of the gospel of the Lord." (1 Nephi 13:24.)

He also saw in vision that this sacred book which we know as the Bible was challenged by the world and that as a result many

of the plain teachings of the Bible "and also many covenants of
the Lord have they taken away . . . that they might pervert the
right ways of the Lord, that they might blind the eyes and harden
the hearts of the children of men."

Hence, the record continues, "an exceeding great many do
stumble, yea, insomuch that Satan hath great power over them."
(1 Nephi 13:25-29.)

No book has suffered the onslaughts which have been leveled
at the Bible, but it has withstood them all, and still is the world's
best seller in the field of literature and religion.

The Bible remains unscathed, but many of its readers do not.
As Nephi's vision indicates, many stumble and fall into the power
of Satan. That can only mean one thing — anti-Christ with all its
attendant evils is at work.

Although the Bible "proceeded forth from the mouth of a
Jew," it is sad to note that some of its worst critics are Jews themselves. In the name of scholarship these men have joined with the
unbelieving but destructive non-Jews in branding the scripture as
myths, as unreliable history and as a conglomeration of writings
from unidentified sources, being questionable from every standpoint.

Surely Nephi's vision is fulfilled in them all. And most truly
have these assaults taken a heavy toll among readers of the scripture, allowing Satan to obtain great power over them.

Latter-day Saints need not become victims of these unholy
critics. The wisdom of God makes foolishness of the supposed
wisdom of men as the Lord reveals his truth through his servants
the prophets.

How blessed we are to have prophets in our midst "to guide
us in these latter days." Our modern prophets are as divinely
chosen and directed as were Moses and Jeremiah.

By revelation we know that the scriptures are from God.
By revelation we know that all creation came by the divine will;
that Adam and Eve were real persons; that there was a Garden of
Eden; there was a Fall and a redemption; there was a flood, with
Noah and his ark.

Revelation is not to be compared to the deductions of men,
no matter how scholarly they appear to be. Revelation is unerring;
it is direct and it is dependable.

Revelation is with us again. Prophets once more minister in the earth. We have modern divine assurance that holy writ is of God and may be read with great benefit to our souls.

The teachings of men — ever so scholarly in appearance — should not divert us from the straight and narrow way.

WHAT SAVES A NATION?

Both George Washington and Abraham Lincoln firmly believed in God. They also believed just as firmly that without God the United States can never survive.

Said Washington in his first inaugural address:

"We ought to be persuaded that the propitious smiles of heaven can never be expected on a nation that disregards the eternal rules of order and right which heaven itself has ordained."

As he addressed both houses of Congress on April 30, 1789, Washington said: "No people can be bound to acknowledge and adore the Invisible Hand which conducts the affairs of men more than the people of the United States. Every step by which they have advanced to the character of an independent nation seems to have been distinguished by some token of Providential agency."

At the time of the surrender of Cornwallis, he spoke of the "reiterated and astonishing interposition of Providence" which had brought victory to the Americans.

He thus recognized the source of our freedom, but he knew full well that only our continued allegiance to that divine source can keep us free.

In the midst of the Civil War, Lincoln recognized the need of Americans to repent of their individual and collective sins. He asked every citizen to humble himself and plead to God for forgiveness as a means of preserving the nation. (Proclamation dated March 30, 1863.)

These expressions are fully in harmony with those made by the prophets of God regarding America. The Book of Mormon is explicit in declaring that this nation will be free only if she will serve the God of this land who is Jesus Christ. (Ether 2:12.)

This warning was repeated from the time of Lehi to the days of Moroni, and the history of the people demonstrated its truth. When they served God they prospered. When they departed from him, destruction came upon them. This situation still faces America today.

When both our government leaders and our prophets tell us the same thing, shall we not respond? In blunt terms, it is: "Repent and survive, or sin and reap destruction."

President Kimball was asked what can bring us peace. He reiterated what the prophets before him had said. Only righteousness can bring us peace, he said.

Crime and wickedness in general are skyrocketing. It is the worst kind of an omen for the future. Shall we not unitedly and individually recognize the handwriting on the wall, for such it is, and take the necessary steps to save ourselves?

It may be all well and good to praise the names of Lincoln and Washington, as it may be to garnish the tombs of the prophets, but if we do not what they say — if we violate the rules of truth and right — what can we expect but the whirlwind?

TO REPLACE PRAYER

Dr. John W. Gilbaugh, professor of education at San Jose State College, raises an interesting question. In a nationally syndicated article he calls attention to the spread of what he calls humanism, and asks: "Have the secular public schools become temples for a religious minority, the humanists?"

He defines humanism as a non-theistic religion, that is, a religion without God. He asserts that some public schools, being restricted by the Supreme Court from allowing nondenominational prayers in their buildings, have now gone over to no-theism.

Most thinking people demand separation of church and state. Most of them likewise willingly agree that all should have the right to worship God according to their own desires, or to go without worship and without God if they so desire. But to allow publicly owned and sponsored institutions to teach that there is no God while they denounce divine faith is quite a different matter.

For years some young people have come out of college with their faith in God shattered, convinced that the Bible is a myth, and that all religion is but an outgrowth of superstition.

Philosophy classes in particular, but others sometimes equally so, have been guilty of destroying faith. Science is often quoted in support of these destructive forces, but only pseudo or outdated scientific hypotheses can be relied on for this. True and great scientists are generally devout men, their own research having convinced them that there is a God, an intelligent being who is in fact the Creator of all things.

The question raised by Dr. Gilbaugh is a very real one. Why should an institution supported by public funds be allowed to destroy faith in God while at the same time forbidding any mention of the positive side of the question? Are public officials willing to allow it? Are they willing to align themselves with no-theism? Why should they allow atheistic teachers to destroy faith without raising one finger to prevent it? Why do they tolerate such a one-sided condition?

No one wants denominationalism taught in public schools. That would violate all facets of freedom of worship. But neither do parents want to support teachers who undermine all they have taught their children from infancy. A teacher has no more right to destroy faith than he has to teach denominationalism in a public school. The rule should work both ways. If faith is not to be taught, then neither should atheism be advocated in our schools.

In the trend toward humanism that is so apparent in the nation, one is reminded of the teaching of the Savior with respect to this subject:

"Whoso shall offend one of these little ones *which believe in me,* it were better for him that a millstone were hanged about his neck, and that he were drowned in the depth of the sea." (Matthew 18:6. Italics added.)

And then he added: "Woe unto the world because of offences! for it must needs be that offences come; but woe to that man by whom the offence cometh!" (Matthew 18:7.)

The evidence to prove that God does live is overwhelming. From scientific research, archaeology and sacred literature, it far outweighs all arguments to the contrary. Is it any wonder that some of the truly wise ones have said that it would require much greater credulity to believe the arguments against God than to accept the sound evidence in his favor?

Faith will long outlast atheism.

Prayer will always be the soul's sincere desire.

If schools cannot teach religion, let them refuse also to teach atheism.

THE RIGHT TO DISAGREE

"It takes all kinds to make a world," some sage once remarked. And it is true. But why are there so many kinds of people? Because God gave us all free agency, the right of self-determination. We are free to choose the way we will go, up or down, or right or left, or we can stay as we are if that is our wish.

We can do as we please in this life, but we must always remember that we must take the consequences for our acts. We reap as we sow. But are we really free in all things? Can we actually attain our ends in any way we please?

We have the right of choice, it is true, and we have the right to disagree with others as much as we please, but there are certain matters which we cannot change no matter how much we wish to do so. There are many things in this life that are not subject to the whims of any man.

We can't change the tides, we can't changes the seasons, we can't change the fact that H_2O is water, or that gravity has a definite attraction. And we can't change the requirements of the gospel.

The Lord is everlasting, unchangeable, the same yesterday, today and tomorrow. And so is his way of saving souls. We are free to disagree with his requirements, and take the consequences, but we are not able to alter the conditions of salvation.

This is a lesson that all mankind must learn. We must come in at the Lord's gate. We must accept his conditions of salvation. If we do not like them, or disagree with them, there is always the opportunity to repent, but if we seek the Lord's blessings, we must obtain them in the Lord's way, and not according to any private notions we may have.

This pertains to sustaining our bishops and other officers of the Church; it has to do with our rejection of false teachers and false doctrines; it has to do with our acceptance of our home teachers, our auxiliary leaders, our baptism and confirmation, our ordination to the priesthood, our obtaining temple recommends; in fact, all phases of the gospel.

When people decide to disagree with the established pattern of the Church, they must realize that they thereby disagree with the Lord, and raise a barrier against themselves in their attainment of salvation.

We are to accept the Church, with its authorized officers, as the pathways to salvation, and humble ourselves sufficiently to overcome any diverse private opinions of our own.

In salvation it is impossible to "agree to disagree," for to disagree with the plan of salvation is to raise a barrier against ourselves.

8.

WOMANHOOD AND MOTHERHOOD

THE CHILD'S ANCHOR

"Hi, Mom, what's for dinner?"

Whether he is of school or preschool age, every child has a natural need for a good home base, an anchor to which he can tie, an unfailing, constant and reliable source of confidence.

Take that away and what becomes of his sense of stability?

When God gave each child its birth, he also provided this anchor in the form of parents and home. He gave to the parents the responsibility to so direct and train their little ones that they might grow up with a sense of security and with a dependable example of righteous living.

But what has become of that anchor? If parents abdicate their responsibility, what happens to the child?

It is estimated that in this nation at least six million little tots under six years of age are left by working mothers either in day-care centers, with relatives, with hired help, with other children, or are left alone during each working day.

More than fifty government agencies are now providing tax funds to care for only a fraction of these youngsters.

It is estimated that more than a quarter of a million small children are cared for by other children or are left alone by working mothers. But even among children left at many day-care centers, the neglect is found to be appalling.

In terms of proper training in health and sanitary habits, what are these little ones given?

What do they receive in motherly love and tenderness, so vital to a small child?

What happens to the setting of ideals and standards of good character?

What examples in righteous living — or its opposite — do children have in other children who may be equally untrained and poorly directed?

What will be the ultimate result in crime or laziness or irresponsibility?

This year the government will spend nearly a billion and a half dollars in various types of child-care projects. Even more is allocated for next year. These funds may not be intended to emancipate mothers from caring for their own children, or to take away the child's primary and God-given anchor in his tender years, but is that becoming the end result?

What a cost in taxes, we might say. But what a greater cost in neglected child development! What a cost too in future problems that may take even more millions in police protection, judicial expense and prison maintenance!

"Hi, Mom, what's for dinner?"

THE NOBILITY OF WOMEN

Latter-day Saint women need not be confused by the philosophical teachings of people who would change the direction of their lives. Of course Latter-day Saints believe in freedom. Of course they believe in liberation from anything that enslaves. Of course they believe in the betterment of every woman and of every man. But are all changes for the better? Are all of the various philosophies that are thrust upon us safe and beneficial?

Inspired direction is available for the women of this Church through the advice of the prophets of God. If their teachings are followed, joy will be the lot of every member.

Said President McKay at one time: "A beautiful, modest, gracious woman is Creation's masterpiece! When with these virtues a woman possesses as guiding stars in her life righteousness and godliness, and an irresistible impulse and desire to make others happy, no one will question if she be classed among those who are truly great."

At another time this inspired leader said: "The highest ideal for our young girls today, as for our mothers who crossed the plains, is love as it may be expressed in marriage and home-building. This virtue, in which love finds true expression, is based upon the spiritual and not the physical side of our being.

"If marriage and home-building are based upon physical attraction alone, love will sooner or later become famished and home life a heavy, disheartening existence."

Is not this the answer?

HONOR AND RESPONSIBILITY

Women enjoy their greatest honor when they accept the God-given responsibility of motherhood. No greater trust is given than bringing spirits into this world. No greater responsibility is placed than to nurture and love a tiny baby. It is important that a baby arrives wanted and cherished in a home where a mother's love exists; where, with the father's love, a family is established; and where, with righteous living, the privileges of motherhood can continue through the eternities.

The responsibility of motherhood begins long before the birth of a child. It begins with a virtuous life to insure a background of purity, respectability and honor before God.

The responsibility involves preparation in the skills and arts of motherhood. These attributes should be learned from youth, and should be taught in a wonderful home by a loving mother. They should include the skills of homemaking and the art of noble living.

Mothers are responsible for a lifetime of preparation and gospel study, and then they are responsible for a lifetime of teaching their children, by precept and example, the precious saving principles.

There is a responsibility in accepting a mate. The eternal joys of motherhood are dependent on a proper marriage, where the priesthood is shared and the labors of the family are the work of the Lord.

Mothers have a role in safeguarding the family from temptation, in teaching children to pray or to repent.

A mother's love, like God's love, should set the tone of Christian living in the home. As that love goes forth it is embraced by the children and is reflected in the family.

There is great honor in motherhood, but there is also a great responsibility.

MOTHER'S HOLY CALLING

President Spencer W. Kimball, addressing a general conference of the Church, gave great emphasis to the sacred role of mothers.

Mothers are partners of God, first in giving righteous birth to the Lord's spirit children as they come into this world, and then in rearing those children so that they will serve the Lord and keep his commandments. There is no more sacred trust.

As President Kimball spoke of the holy role of mothers, he preceded what he said with a strong appeal for the virtuous life, and said, "We reaffirm our strong, unalterable stand against unchastity in all its manifestations."

After saying that all mothers have a sacred role to fill, he quoted from a statement previously issued by the First Presidency giving great emphasis to this point:

"Motherhood thus becomes a holy calling, a sacred dedication for carrying out the Lord's plans, a consecration of devotion to the uprearing and fostering, the nurturing in body, mind, and spirit, of those who kept their first estate and who come to this earth for their second estate 'to see if they will do all things whatsoever the Lord their God shall command them.' (Abraham 3:25.)

"To lead them to keep their second estate is the work of motherhood, and 'they who keep their second estate shall have glory added upon their heads for ever and ever.'

"This divine service of motherhood can be rendered only by mothers. It may not be passed to others. Nurses cannot do it; public nurseries cannot do it; hired help cannot do it — only mother, aided as much as may be by the loving hands of father, brothers, and sisters, can give the full needed measure of watchful care.

"The mother who entrusts her child to the care of others, that she may do non-motherly work, whether for gold, for fame, or for civic service, should remember that 'a child left to himself bringeth his mother to shame.' (Proverbs 29:15.)

"In our day the Lord has said that unless parents teach their children the doctrines of the church, 'the sin be upon the heads of the parents.' (D&C 68:25.)

"Motherhood is near to divinity. It is the highest, holiest service to be assumed by mankind. It places her who honors its holy calling and service next to the angels.

"To you mothers in Israel we say, God bless and protect you, and give you the strength and courage, the faith and knowledge, the holy love and consecration to duty, that shall enable you to fill to the fullest measure the sacred calling which is yours.

"To you mothers and mothers-to-be we say: Be chaste, keep pure, live righteously, that your posterity to the last generation may call you blessed."

When President McKay spoke of motherhood, he said another striking thing. "Next to eternal life, the most precious gift that our Father in heaven can bestow upon mankind is his children."

And then he added: "There are three fundamental things to which every child is entitled: first, a respected name, second, a sense of security; and third, opportunities for development."

Good parents should provide all of these.

A MOTHER'S GOAL

For years we have celebrated Mother's Day. It has been almost sacred in its observance. It has come on Sunday when our minds are most closely attuned to the Holy Spirit, and it has been a reminder that motherhood indeed is akin to godhood.

We have reminded ourselves over and over again that human beings are the spirit offspring of God, and that it is a special privilege for mothers to usher into this world the children of the Almighty.

Hence, Mother's Day has been a sacred and loving day when the good mothers of the land have been recognized properly for what they are, and when we, the children, have again pledged our fealty to those who gave us birth.

But what should be the major thrust of our observance? Of course we will honor our mothers. Of course we will thank them and love them for all they have done for us, giving us life and rearing us so that we might have joy in that life. This we must always do.

But also we must recognize that the very institution of virtuous and true motherhood is being severely — even frighteningly — challenged today. The kind of motherhood which God provided is being jeopardized. Some influences would destroy home and family. Some go so far as to advocate the elimination of marriage, but that is only among the extremists.

Still others, however, are attempting to "liberate" mothers from both home and children so that they may seek careers or added income in industry and other types of employment.

Day-care centers by the thousands are being set up. Rearing of little ones is given to hired help having no personal interest. An immediate result of much of this is a wave of emotional problems among the children themselves. There is widespread parental neglect. Juvenile delinquency rising so fast is directly related to the ground swell of the new psychology.

Once we destroy the real image of true motherhood, we take a great step toward the utter destruction of the home. Destroy good homes having wholesome family life, and we step onto the threshold of uprooting our national foundations.

All of this, of course, is related also to the growing atheism which is sweeping the world, as God is downgraded, doubted and defied; as even little school children are taught that our origin, instead of being divine, is but earthy, a part of an alleged evolutionary process which found its beginnings in chemicals, microorganisms, fish and other low orders of life. All of this tends to eliminate God and his special creation, and destroy faith in the divine concept that we are literally his offspring.

Motherhood must be re-enshrined as the holy institution which the Almighty conceived it to be. Once again we must realize that there is a God in heaven, that we are his children, and that he himself established motherhood on its virtuous and elevated plane.

Every God-fearing, God-believing person must contribute to that sacred concept by increasing his own faith in God, by honoring true motherhood, by never stooping to the destruction of virtue, and by protecting the family as a divinely established institution.

As God lives, so must the family concept be preserved and this can be done by cherishing true motherhood.

WHERE OBLIGATION STOPS

A mother of several children was interviewed by her bishop. The husband and father of this family had gone astray and was in the act of joining one of the small dissident groups advocating apostate doctrines.

The mother loved the Church. She also, of course, loved her husband and children. But she did not believe the apostate doctrines which her husband had espoused.

She had hoped to keep her family together. She had prayed that her husband's dissidence would not mean a break-up of the family. The children needed a father as well as a mother. They also needed the Church, as did the whole family.

As the mother studied the situation, she knew that if her husband continued in his association with apostates that he would become one of them and would be excommunicated from the Church. She knew that if she followed him into the dissident group, the children would come with them. Then they would become apostate as they grew up.

In prayer she pondered what her course should be. Should she follow her husband into the cult, and be excommunicated herself? What would that do her eternal salvation? If the children should follow them into the cult, would they also lose their salvation? Isn't it a fact that salvation is found only in the Church, and not in dissident groups?

Where did her greatest loyalty lie? To her husband, in one direction, or to the Church, to herself, and her children in the opposite way? Since she was married to her husband, and had promised to "love, honor and obey," did that covenant overrule all else?

Then she remembered President Harold B. Lee and his teachings in a Relief Society lesson. He had taught that wives need not follow their husbands into sin and disobedience, but that they were obliged to obey their husbands only in righteousness.

She looked up the Relief Society lesson and read from an address by President Lee the following:

"In defining the relationship of a wife to her husband, the late President George Albert Smith put it this way: 'In showing this relationship, by a symbolic representation, God didn't say that woman was to be taken from a bone in the man's head that she should rule over him, nor from a bone in his foot that she should be trampled under his feet, but from a bone in his side to symbolize that she was to stand by his side, to be his companion, his equal, and his helpmeet in all their lives together.'

"I fear some husbands have interpreted erroneously the statement that the husband is to be the head of the house and that his wife is to obey the law of her husband. Brigham Young's instructions to husbands was this: 'Let the husband and father learn to bend his will to the will of his God, and then instruct . . . in this lesson of self-government by his example as well as by his precept.' (*Discourses of Brigham Young* [Deseret Book Co., 1925], pp. 306, 307.)

"This is but another way of saying that the wife is to obey the law of her husband only as he obeys the laws of God. No woman is expected to follow her husband in disobedience to the commandments of the Lord."

WEIGHING THE VALUES

To work or not to work is a question facing a great many mothers in these days of "liberation," and especially among those who regard home and family as impediments and encumbrances. And then, too, the matter is often entirely economic. Shall they work to obtain a higher standard of living, or shall they be content with less?

Always the children come into the picture, and with them the basic responsibilities of motherhood.

Can women place their children in commercial day-care centers with an assurance that in those places the little ones will be given the kind of love and understanding that only a mother can give? Should they be content with less? Can they feel content that children left with relatives will receive the kind of care a conscientious mother would give? Is less than that acceptable?

If they are left with older children, even in the same family, will the little ones again be deprived of that which only a mother can give? Would the loss in training be fully compensated for by the few extra dollars that would be added to the family income?

In these days when the fundamental responsibilities of being a mother are depreciated and even challenged, what should the wise mother do? She might ask herself a few questions that come close to the heart:

Does the family really need the added income? After all, money cannot buy happiness.

What will it cost the child in terms of character-building, faith-building, and a sense of security?

What really is most important in life? Did not the Lord say it was to save souls? And can souls be saved by remote control or without education in the standards of right and wrong, or by some public agency?

Who can best teach those standards? An agency? Another child? An aunt or a grandma? Or is it the mother, she who is appointed to this responsibility by heaven itself?

The Church has always been the world's foremost advocate of feminine rights and women's happiness. It recognizes what the "equal rights" laws say, of course, and reasserts its stand that we believe in honoring, upholding and sustaining the law. But it also holds high the divine responsibilities given to women by the Lord himself. And is there anything greater?

To use the language of the First Presidency:

"The leaders of the Church have consistently taught that mothers who have young children in the home should devote their primary energies to the companionship and training of their children and care of their families, and should not seek employment outside the home unless there is no other way that the family's basic needs can be provided.

"As we view the distressing conditions in our society, many of which we attribute to the weakening of influences of the home, we earnestly desire that all members of The Church of Jesus Christ of Latter-day Saints — as well as all persons everywhere — would follow this counsel."

WHEN MOTHERS WORK

What is the working mother doing to the homes of our country?
Is the added income worth the adverse effect such employment
has on the family?

One study was made in which it was learned that 25 percent
of the children of working mothers have emotional or discipline
problems. The study revealed also that in families where the
mother does not go out to work only 10 percent of the children are
so afflicted.

In national studies some very sad conditions have been
revealed. Some little children are locked in their homes for the
day when the mother leaves for work in the morning, and are
left there alone until she returns in the evening. Some homes have
been set on fire by these youngsters as they played with matches.

In other instances, social workers have found that children
are locked out of their homes by their mothers, and must remain
outside until the mother returns in the evening. In this group,
delinquency is very high.

Clandestine courtships in places of employment have broken
up some homes; in others where "swing shifts" are worked by both
husband and wife, the home loses its continuity, and what do the
children do then?

When our situation reaches a point where women prefer to
work, even at the risk of their marriages and the stability of their
children, we have stumbled into a sad plight indeed.

Every mother should look the facts squarely in the face and
ask if the job is really worth what it costs. Added income may
look good, but can it compensate for the adverse effect it has on
the home?

PRESERVING FEMININITY

In the beginning God made men as males and women as females
and he had good reason for doing so. He expected men to be
masculine and do the type of work their bodies were naturally

suited for. Likewise he made women to suit their role in life, which was utterly different from that of men.

Why do people continually try to change nature? Were women intended to be stevedores, bricklayers, carpenters, road construction workers and coal miners? Are not women ignominiously downgraded by any willingness to have them do such work? Where is the femininity with which God blessed them?

But putting women in men's jobs is not the only handicap they draw down upon their unsuspecting heads in this new effort. There is the problem of their home life, their marriages, and their children. Herein are the greatest problems.

We are told that working women will add greatly to the family income, and that they can then buy more and more home conveniences and enjoy a more affluent life.

Children, it is said, may be placed in child-care centers, and for doing so Uncle Sam will pay mothers $4,800 per year.

But what becomes of the home influence to which every child is entitled? Can the hired staff in a day-care center provide the tender motherly care so needed to make children good and help them to grow up to become solid citizens? Seventy-seven percent of these centers have been declared substandard by the Child Welfare League.

The great danger of women accepting the new psychology is not so much the ridiculous idea that they can do cement work and mine coal, but it is that our already frightful child neglect problems, our juvenile delinquency, and our broken marriages will be skyrocketing.

Haven't we had enough of child neglect? Don't we have enough divorce in this country without developing a formula which is certain to make more? Aren't children worthy of proper rearing? What about their rights? What mother has the right to impose severe handicaps upon a growing child?

Women's rights! What about women's responsibilities? Can they abdicate them with impunity in the midst of this ground swell of political fallacy?

God intended women to be good mothers, and motherhood in more than the reproductive process. Motherhood means training children properly and giving them the love they require for psychological and spiritual balance, a thing which no hired help can provide.

Of course women can go out and try to do men's work if they insist, but the children will pay for it with emotional and delinquency problems. The whole nation likewise will suffer as we then shall develop a handicapped new generation such as we have never before seen in America. Who then can count the ultimate cost?

EQUAL RIGHTS AMENDMENT

On April 28, 1842, the Prophet Joseph Smith, following organization of the Relief Society, declared: "I now turn the key in your [women's] behalf in the name of the Lord. . . . And this society shall rejoice, and knowledge and intelligence shall flow down [upon women] from this time henceforth."

With this declaration, when women's organizations were almost nonexistent, the Prophet placed the Church in the forefront of those who have taught the dignified and exalted place of women. To this end Church leaders from those early times have advocated programs to enhance the status of women as daughters of God. They have also actively given encouragement and support to legislative measures designed to safeguard the welfare of women, the home and the family.

Over a period of many decades, women have been accorded special protection and the status properly due them. More recently, these include equality of opportunity in political, civil and economic spheres.

But now there are many who feel that the way to take care of inequities that may have existed in the past, or may presently exist, is to ratify the Equal Rights Amendment to the Constitution. Legislators in a number of states have been or will be faced with decisions on this question.

Both Mrs. Belle S. Spafford, former president of the nearly one-million-member, worldwide Relief Society of the Church, and her successor, Mrs. Barbara B. Smith, have spoken forthrightly on this question, the former in a widely published interview with George W. Cornell, religion editor of the Associated Press; the latter in a talk before the University of Utah Institute of Religion. Among their statements were these:

"It appears that the Equal Rights Amendment is not only imperfect, but dangerous."

"The blanket approach of the Equal Rights Amendment is a confused step backward in time, instead of a clear stride into the future."

"The Equal Rights Amendment is not the way. It . . . will not fulfill their hopes, but rather would work to the disadvantage of both women and men."

It "is so broad that it is inadequate, inflexible, and vague; so all-encompassing that it is nondefinitive."

Legislative hearings and debate have doubtless produced millions of words uttered on both sides with much emotion. But all of this does not change the fact that men and women are different, made so by a Divine Creator. Each has his or her role. One is incomplete without the other.

Out of innate wisdom and the experience of centuries, lawmakers have enacted measures for the benefit and protection of each of the sexes, but more particularly of women. In this country they have already provided statutory equality of opportunity in political, civil, and economic affairs. If this has not always been extended, it has usually been the result of lack of enforcement rather than absence of law.

The writer of the lead story in the January 1975 issue of the prestigious *Nation's Business* summarized a thorough presentation of the case with these words concerning the Equal Rights Amendment:

"The amendment is unnecessary.

"The amendment is uncertain.

"The amendment is undesirable."

He concluded by saying, "It seems to me highly doubtful that the people desire any such thing as 'unisex' in their law. But if five more states ratify the pending amendment, that is what the people will get."

FAMILIES WILL SURVIVE

"Motherhood and the sanctity of the home will survive all attacks being made upon them." So affirmed then President Belle S. Spafford of the Relief Society of the Church in an address given before a distinguished group in New York City.

"I am convinced," she said, "that the home will stand as it has stood during past generations, as the cornerstone of a good society and a happy citizenry.

"While old activity patterns within the home may be modified by the impact of change outside the home, the enduring values which cannot be measured in terms of their monetary worth, their power for good, the need of the human being for them — such values as peace, security, love, understanding — will not be sacrificed on the altar of new philosophies and new concepts."

President Spafford further asserted: "Countless men and women and even children who have tasted these fruits of home and family life will recognize new philosophies which create spoilage in them and they will fend them off.

"It is in the home that the lasting values of life are best internalized in the individual. It is this which builds good citizens, and good citizens make good nations."

She reviewed the history of women's movements in the world, and pointed out that The Church of Jesus Christ of Latter-day Saints has been in advance of other movements promoting the cause of women, beginning with the organization of the Relief Society by the Prophet Joseph Smith in 1842, and the granting of the right to vote within the Church from its founding. Women, as men, vote on new officers and other changes in the various organizations of the Church.

Sister Spafford was given a standing ovation at the conclusion of her address, which was later quoted widely in the public press. She is recognized as one of the great women of the world, and has held leading positions in world women's organizations. She has served two terms as president of the National Council of Women of the United States. Throughout her life she has been a devoted Latter-day Saint, a true mother, and a power for good among women.

From her vantage point, she can see in clear perspective the true and exalted position of mothers and of all women in the divine plan of God, and is its firm advocate.

9.

MARRIAGE
AND
FAMILY

THE REAL TEACHERS

The television has replaced both parent and teacher as the primary educator of children. So declared Dr. Gerald Looney of the University of Arizona, in addressing the American Academy of Pediatrics.

The learned doctor, who has made a nationwide study of this subject over a period of many months, says that the average pre-school child spends 64 percent of his time watching TV.

By the time the child is fourteen he will have seen eighteen thousand murders on television, and by the time he reaches seventeen he will have listened to three hundred fifty thousand commercials.

Constant watching of movies in which violence is the main theme, involving robberies, courtroom scenes, drunken brawls and seduction, shapes his mind and builds a distorted conception of what life really is, the learned doctor says. Some may not agree he admits, but this is what the "primary educator" really does to the child.

Should anything replace the instruction by parents in the home? All will readily say no, but the fact remains that various other factors do just that. Partially responsible for this is the fact that numerous parents no longer acknowledge their natural responsibility to their children, and are too interested in their own selfish pleasures and pursuits to be concerned about their offspring.

Thousands are now patronizing day-care centers for children, centers which operate at night as well, often relieving parents of all responsibility for their children except the matter of paying the "tuition."

Coupled with this are reports of increased child abuse, in some instances so severe that little helpless infants are actually beaten to death by their enraged parents, who haven't the patience to listen to their crying.

If they didn't want children, why did they send for them? The true answer of course is: they didn't. They wanted only gratification, not offspring.

Values of many persons are beginning to fall to new lows. Pleasure-seeking takes the place of responsibility; ease supplants effort; voluptuous living replaces the kind of life which made our Lincolns, Washingtons and Jeffersons and their associates who laid the foundations of a sound democracy.

It has been said quite often that no nation can survive which allows the destruction of its homes. This is verily true. Is it any wonder then that the thinking part of the populace now begins to fear for its own future as more and more parents seem to take steps toward the dissolution of the family?

The home evening program of the Church deserves even greater emphasis under conditions such as these. Latter-day Saints understand that home life on earth is but a prelude to family life in eternity. Our whole religion is based upon the concept that God is our Father and we are his family. As we are commanded to become like him, we too must cherish our family life and make of it the most wholesome and enjoyable influence that comes into the lives of our children.

And what is to be the basis of our type of family life? Spirituality! Latter-day Saint homes must be gospel-centered. There we teach and live the gospel. There we develop family ties which should never be broken. There children should be taught to respect their parents, their brothers and sisters, and themselves.

Understanding should be the watchword between parents and children, and that does not come by remote control. Neither does it come via the television set, nor through day-care centers, nor other "baby-sitting" activities.

It comes through the loving, constant, ever-present and personal care of children by their parents, based always on mutual love and cooperation between the parents themselves.

Love at home is the goal for Latter-day Saints, and it comes through love of God, which in turn can develop only as we serve him with all our heart, might, mind and strength.

OUR LEARNING PROCESS

The school is not the only center of education for the modern world. Important as it is, it nevertheless is incomplete without two other great sources of learning: the home and the church.

This is likely what led Dr. T. H. Bell, former U.S. Commissioner of Education, to say: "Not everything worth knowing is learned in school. And unfortunately not everything learned in school is worth knowing."

No one can truly measure the value of proper learning, for it can mold character, direct careers, and establish moral and spiritual values without which there can be no successful life.

The home is the basic unit of society, with the church and the school closely related in one grand triumvirate. Each is vitally needed, each is independent in its own sphere, and each has a God-given mission to fulfill.

There is no thought on the part of right-thinking people to allow any one of these three factors to dominate the others. Each is to be independent in its own right, but one of them should never be allowed to disrupt the wholesome influence of the others.

If it ever became necessary to abolish any of the three, however, the home must survive, for it could become both a school and a house of worship. A good home is basic to the growth of civilization.

Abraham Lincoln did pretty well in his early life without either school or church. He had a mother who took care of the complete situation in her limited way.

Today, when we have so many facilities, we need all three of these factors. In each there must be taught those vital principles without which there can be no good character, no strong nation, no great civilization.

In this day when standards are slipping so fast that it takes away our breath, thoughtful parents must look to their responsibility in all three of these fields. They must first and foremost build strong homes, fostering good morals and high standards of conduct. They must hold to the Church. It was the Lord who said that we must seek first the kingdom of God and his righteousness, with the promise that other needful things will be given to us.

We must take so active a part in the education of our children that they will be taught what they need for success in the world, beginning with the three Rs. We can help avoid the teaching of hypotheses in science and social subjects which are destructive of the faith and morals taught to these same youngsters in church and home. The school must be the ally of the home and the church, but never their antagonist.

HAVING A FAMILY

In 1975 *U.S. News & World Report* published results of national surveys showing that "nearly all women want to marry and raise a family." How refreshing this is in the wake of publicity and campaigns to the contrary!

The yearning for motherhood is as natural for a woman as it is for her to breathe. It is born in her; it is a divine attribute; it is part of the purpose of her creation.

Trends against marriage and family life are contrary to the revelations of God, and men and women alike who violate the purpose of matrimony must some day account to the Almighty for their actions.

It was President David O. McKay who said: "America seems to be drifting toward a low level as regards the law of family and home, with the result that sin and crime are increasing to an alarming extent."

He then continued: "The exalted view of marriage as held by this Church is given expressly in five words in section 49 of the Doctrine and Covenants: *'Marriage is ordained of God'*."

And then he gives this advice: "It is your duty and mine to uphold the lofty conception of marriage as given in this revelation and to guard against encroaching dangers that threaten to lower the standards of the ideal home." (*Gospel Ideals,* pp. 462-463.)

What is marriage for? "Marriage is for the purpose of rearing a family. Failure to do so is one of the conditions that causes love to wilt and eventually die. . . .

"The purpose of marriage is to bear children and rear a family. . . . I repeat that the very purpose of marriage is to rear a family and not for the mere gratification of man or woman." (*Ibid.*, pp. 466-467.)

President Joseph F. Smith sustained this position wholeheartedly. Said he: "Marriage is the preserver of the human race. Without it the purposes of God would be frustrated. . . . No man who is of marriageable age is living his religion who remains single." (*Gospel Doctrine*, p. 273.)

And then says President Smith: "I think it is a crying evil that there should exist a sentiment or feeling among any members of the Church to curtail the birth of their children. I think it is a crime wherever it occurs, where husband and wife are free from impurities that would be entailed upon their posterity." (*Ibid.*, p. 278.)

Like all other citizens, Latter-day Saints are bombarded with the philosophical meanderings of persons who would limit families, provide free contraceptives even to teenagers, and endorse abortions. But as in all other things, we must remember that "there must needs be an opposition in all things," and that we are to follow the law of God and not the contrary teachings of man.

In this matter, once again we are at the crossroads. Shall we follow the philosophers, or shall we follow God's inspired prophets?

LIKE FATHER, LIKE SON

There is an old saying: "Like mother, like daughter; like father, like son."

Children do resemble their parents as a general rule, because the parents become their examples in life, whether for good or for bad.

It is a fact that drinking parents nearly always have drinking children; smoking parents nearly always have smoking children; dishonest parents have dishonest children; well-trained parents nearly always — with very few exceptions — have well-trained children.

It is even true in religion and politics. Catholic parents usually have Catholic children; protestant parents usually have protestant children. Republican parents usually have Republican children, and Democrat parents usually have Democrat children.

Parents are the prime example for their children.

Quarreling parents have quarreling children. Careless parents have careless children. If there is no discipline, no proper training in the home, children will never know the meaning of discipline, nor will they receive the kind of training that makes them worthwhile citizens.

Parents who say they are sick of their children, that the "kids are too much trouble," need not blame their little ones too much if the children are riotous and disobedient.

Are the parents themselves obedient? Are they hard to get along with? Are they respectful of the law? Is there order in the home? Parents set the pattern, consciously or otherwise. And nearly always the children follow that pattern. So if parents are "disillusioned" in the matter of having a family, instead of blaming the children they should take a good hard look at themselves.

There is also another element — again determined by the parents. There is nothing like the gospel of Christ to bring love and harmony into the home. If parents would truly have a successful family, they must introduce the gospel into the home, and make it the rule of life. Everyone will then be happy with everyone else.

HOME AND FAMILY

Preservation of home and family is one of our highest duties, and yet mankind seems to be drifting away from the lofty concepts of those sacred institutions. They are sacred. They are intended to be forever. They were instituted by the Lord himself, and were intended to have eternal significance. They are part of his plan for our progress both here and hereafter. They are as essential as any other part of the gospel. Our very exaltation is based largely upon our acceptance of the principles of true family life.

Most people do not realize or understand that in the Lord's plan of salvation, the man is not without the woman and the woman is not without the man in the Lord. (1 Corinthians 11:11.) But that is not all. Just as the Lord commands marriage, he likewise commands that within that marriage children are to be reared.

We are to give bodies to his spirit children: We should make those children welcome in our homes. We should rear them in the gospel. We should be missionaries to them and purposefully convert them to the gospel so that it may become a saving power in their lives.

It is expected that they, in turn, will follow our examples and do likewise, thus developing generations of faithful and believing souls who will be willing to help build the kingdom of God on earth and prepare for the kingdom of heaven which is to follow. Thus we may fulfill the command the Lord gave us in the Sermon on the Mount to perfect ourselves, even as our Father which is in heaven is perfect.

Since God is our Father, and we are commanded to be like him, our efforts in that direction must be our first consideration. He and his purposes must come first in our lives. Our great objective is to serve him and mold our lives in the gospel pattern. It is the pattern of perfection.

President McKay used to teach that couples who are blessed with mental and physical vigor are recreant to their duty if they refuse to meet the natural and rightful responsibilities of parenthood. The primary purpose of marriage is the rearing of families. This we must never forget. Every family, of course, will pay due regard to the health and welfare of the mother in this matter.

But a married woman who refuses to assume the responsibilities of motherhood, or, having children, neglects them for pleasure or social prestige, is recreant to the highest calling and privilege of womanhood. So taught President McKay.

And any father who, because of social or business pressures, fails to share with his wife the responsibility of rearing the children is untrue to his marital obligations, President McKay said.

Some men are abusive to their wives and at times use them for physical gratification only, which is most despicable. Self-control, not indulgence, is the evidence of manhood, President McKay taught.

Couples who, in the spirit of the gospel and with due respect for each other, perform the duties of proper marriage, will receive peace in this life, and unmeasured blessings in eternity.

FIDELITY BEGETS FIDELITY

Fidelity in living the gospel is closely related to fidelity in family life. It is a matter of character. Fidelity means faithfulness, loyalty and devotion.

If fidelity prevails in one's heart, he will be true to his trust whether in the home, in business, in the Church, or in any other activity. An honest person is honest wherever he may be.

The following letter has been received from a high priest in California, which is pertinent to this point:

"I am a teacher of a high priests group in which there are fourteen members. In our meeting last Sunday there were ten members present, the other four being assigned to church activities in other departments.

"During our lesson on how to build a happy and successful marriage, I made a survey of the length of time each member had been married. The total number of years involved for the ten members present was 370 years.

"I thought it was a great tribute for a group of men of our Church to have been happily married an average of thirty-seven years. (The average would have been forty except that one of the high priests is a young man who has been married only thirteen years.)

"In this day and age where broken homes and divorce are so prevalent, I thought it remarkable that all of these men were happily married, with all of their wives still living. They were unanimously of the opinion that they were all more in love now than when they were first married."

It is another example of faith and works. It is also another example that faith *does* work when it is applied in our daily lives.

If people would live the gospel, and thus develop Christlike traits of character; if they would take the gospel into their homes, doing to each other as they would be done by; if they would develop a spiritual atmosphere in the home, building faith and good character, they would seldom if ever have any marriage problems.

Has there ever been a divorce unless one or both of the parties concerned violated some principle of the gospel?

Since marital unhappiness reflects selfishness and other violations of Christian principles, the answer must be repentance, not further violation. Repentance is the answer to every broken law of the Lord. Repentance would solve most of our marriage problems.

THOSE BROKEN HOMES

From many parts of the world the Church is receiving high commendation for its efforts to preserve home and family. Government officials, civic leaders, educators and professional counselors have praised the Church for its program.

The home evening program sponsored throughout the Church is being lauded by newspaper and magazine editors as an answer to one of the nation's greatest problems, and it is being imitated by some organized groups which see its great value. What a need there is for it! And what a potent remedy it is for disharmony in the home, for lack of character and religious training, and for delinquency among both youth and adults!

The divorce trend in America becomes steadily more frightening. It seems incredible that while the population of the United States increased only 167 percent from 1900 to 1970, the divorce rate for the same period jumped by 1,177 percent. At the present time, the national divorce rate is one for every three marriages.

Children affected by divorce action also have increased greatly. In 1955 there were 347,000 children involved in such legal proceedings, but within a decade the number had doubled.

Studies indicate that disputes over money comprise the chief cause of divorce. Marrying too young is another primary reason. Six times more divorces occur among persons married under twenty-one than among those who marry above that age. It is appalling.

Other major causes of divorce are repulsive sex practices, in-law interference, conflicting religious affiliations, politics, and lack of affection. Premarital pregnancy is becoming an increasing cause of divorce. It leads to many forced marriages, so few of which survive.

A family counselor, addressing a convention in Utah, said: "Wouldn't it be valuable to require young people to spend at least as much time preparing for a marriage license as they do to qualify for a driver's license?"

He also said, "Marriage is the only profession where one doesn't have to prove competency before entering it."

But think what good homes can do to correct all of these problems! Good homes can teach young people the value of money and how to handle it. Good homes can so educate children that they will gladly avoid child-marriages. Good homes teach virtue, the great fortification against pre-marital intimacies which force so many early marriages and quick divorces.

Proper home life will teach in-laws to mind their own business and allow young couples to work out their own plans. Good homes teach the gospel and bring conversion to the hearts of all members of the family. Then there will be little inclination toward inter-denominational marriages with their subsequent disputes over religion.

Good homes, through spirituality, lay the foundation for peace, harmony and understanding. They teach people how to do unto others as they would be done by.

The gospel is the answer to the broken-home problem and, through the home evening, it may reach its ultimate in successful family life.

DIVORCE INSURANCE

New York legislators and feminists are promoting the idea of divorce insurance. It would be used, according to news dispatches, "to ensure adequate child support in the event of divorce, but could also be used by childless divorced couples, and should the marriage be a lasting one, be converted to other uses."

There is no doubt about the increasing effect of divorce on the nation as the rate of separations continues to soar. And certainly there is no doubt about its adverse influence upon children in every case of separation.

But would not insurance encourage divorce by making it seem easier to bear, and therefore more attractive? How much more important would it be to provide a type of insurance which would prevent divorce in the first place, rather than to serve as a palliative afterward?

And what is such insurance? The Lord gave it to us in the form of the Golden Rule: "All things whatsoever ye would that men should do to you, do ye even so to them." (Matthew 7:12.) He gave it, too, in modern revelation: "Thou shalt love thy wife with all thy heart, and shalt cleave unto her and none else." (D&C 42:22.)

If couples would overcome their selfishness, and bring the gospel into their homes, there would be no need for divorce.

THE HEAD OF THE FAMILY

For some years now, both in and out of the Church, there has been a movement to "put father back as the head of the family." One commentary on the subject is interesting as it came in a letter from a mother:

"Oh, I'm in full agreement that father should be the head of the family. But I resent the assertions that mother has usurped that position. If she is on the throne it isn't because she sought the position. It is because father has abdicated!

"Maybe I know the wrong people, but none of the husbands I know spend much more time at home than is necessary for eating and sleeping.

"If the head of any institution or firm attempted to run his business in the amount of time comparable to what he spends with his children, he would soon lose his position entirely or some other person would have to take over for him and run things. This is precisely what the average wife is doing.

"I love, admire and respect my husband, and I am immensely proud of the work he does. Our six youngsters feel the same way and none of us would dream of questioning his decisions, nor do we challenge his right to make them.

"But the fact remains that he is home for a very, very small percentage of their waking hours, and I am about 99 percent disciplinarian in our home whether I like it or not — and I don't. And neither does any other mother."

'Nuff said!

"I LOVE HIM BEST . . ."

A young mother stood before two thousand people in a general session of her stake conference, and described the home evening programs conducted by her family. She spoke feelingly of her affection for her little ones and then, in most endearing terms, expressed the love and admiration she holds for her husband, the father of her children. She told of his achievements and of the good times he gives them, and then said, "but I love my husband best when he is honoring his priesthood in the home."

She could have said no more expressive thing. What a significant statement! It had a salutary effect upon the audience.

"When he is honoring his priesthood in the home." That statement — when he truly does honor his priesthood in the home — covers virtually the entire scope of the gospel, the full meaning of Latter-day Saint living.

If he truly honors his priesthood both in the home and out, he is fully devoted to the gospel principles which build Christlike traits of character in his own soul, which inspire his children to live righteously as he does, and which teach him to appreciate his wife as a daughter of God. Thereby he establishes "love at home."

Then indeed there is beauty all around, then truly "there is one who smiles on high," for love at home means having the Spirit of Christ in the home, faith and faithfulness in the hearts of all who are there, and the erection of a bastion against "all the fiery darts of the adversary."

Men who honor their priesthood — in the home and out — have what the Lord called "love unfeigned," including "faith, hope, charity and love, with an eye single to the glory of God." They are examples of "faith, virtue, knowledge, temperance, patience, brotherly kindness, godliness, charity, humility, diligence." (D&C 4:5, 6.)

But, let us ask, does any man honor his priesthood — truly — if he does not honor it in the home? Can he be an example of piety outside the home but an unkind wretch within the family circle, and still regard himself as a Christian?

If he honors his priesthood out of the home, to be consistent he certainly must do so within the home also. If he does not honor his priesthood in the home, he can lay no claim to doing so anywhere else.

And if he truly honors his sacred calling, the Lord has said: "all that my Father hath shall be given unto him." (D&C 84:38.) But the priesthood covenant provides the measuring rod when it says that he "shall live by every word that proceedeth forth from the mouth of God." (D&C 84:44.)

VIRTUE IN THE HOME

Certain lecturers with very worldly philosophies are coming into some communities ostensibly talking about harmony in family life. They do talk about such harmony, but only as a preliminary to other matters which are not so innocent.

Their lecture courses include instruction in connubial practices which are abhorrent to right-thinking people, who now come to their Church leaders asking if such things are compatible with the gospel. Many are left in a state of confusion; others not so well oriented accept such teachings and introduce practices into the home which could destroy purity and virtue and undermine the respect which husbands and wives should have for each other. Without such respect, no marriage can be successful.

Right-thinking people must realize that perversions are perversions whether in or out of marriage, and that to introduce filthy practices into their relationships is but to lay the foundation either for divorce or the corruption of good character and spirituality.

Purity of mind and heart are vital to our welfare, but how are we to develop it?

How are we to assure ourselves of answers to our prayers?

How are we to draw near enough to the Lord to make certain that we shall receive of his Holy Spirit?

The Savior gives us the answers in one of his revelations to the Prophet Joseph Smith. Said he in Doctrine and Covenants 121:45:

"Let virtue garnish thy thoughts unceasingly; then shall thy confidence wax strong in the presence of God; and the doctrine of the priesthood shall distil upon thy soul as the dews from heaven."

If we practice such continued virtue in both thought and deed, we are assured that "the Holy Ghost shall be [our] constant companion." (D&C 121:46.)

Perversions are filthy. We must realize that the spirit of God will not dwell in a temple made unclean by sinful practices.

Who of all people are so blessed as to have the Spirit of God to dwell within them? To some extent, the Lord gives his Spirit to every worthy person, but those who have received the gift of the Holy Ghost possess that Spirit in a most special way.

Shall these favored ones defile their tabernacles with perversions taught from some lecture platform?

"Know ye not that ye are the temple of God," Paul asked, "and that the Spirit of God dwelleth in you?" He was talking to members of the Church who had been confirmed and given the gift of the Holy Ghost.

Then he continued: "If any man defile the temple of God, him shall God destroy; for the temple of God is holy, which temple ye are." (1 Corinthians 3:16-17.)

Such individuals became the temple of God's Holy Spirit by joining his church, being baptized, confirmed, and receiving the gift of the Holy Ghost. If members, so blessed, defile themselves, can they hope to retain his Spirit which he has said will not dwell in unclean temples? (Helaman 4:24.)

Paul taught: "Let no man deceive himself" (1 Corinthians 4:18), and the Savior instructed his modern Saints: "Cease to be unclean" (D&C 88:124), and "Keep . . . uncleanness far from you" (D&C 90:18).

The marriage ceremony does not give license for sin and perversion. Married or unmarried, the Lord commands his people to be clean and he said, "Ye must practise virtue and holiness before me *continually."* (D&C 46:33. Italics added.)

Since the thought precedes the act, it is all the more important that we let virtue garnish our thoughts unceasingly.

TO FORM OR TO REFORM?

A 1975 issue of the *National Observer* carried a front-page article entitled "Reform Is a Flop." It referred to reformation of prisoners. The article, written by Michael T. Malloy, said:

"Nothing works. Judges and jailors, cops and robbers, reformers and reactionaries are increasingly coming to the same dismal conclusion about a century and a half of prison reform in the United States. No matter what we do to fight crime by trying to reform criminals, nothing works."

It quoted Judge Philip M. Saeta of Los Angeles: "Long sentences don't make any difference; short sentences don't make any difference; fines don't work any better than jail. Probation — we're still shooting blind."

Former Attorney General William Saxbe was quoted as saying that rehabilitation of criminals is a myth, and a former convict now in the New England Prisoners Association termed prison reform as "a cynical joke with every prisoner I've ever talked with."

The article then went on to say that it isn't that no prisoners are reformed, for many of them are on an individual basis. It is a fact that many people convicted of crimes do repent and change their ways. But it is also true that a high percentage of criminals are repeaters who return to jail time and time again and never reform.

When will we learn that prevention is better than correction? If we had adequate prevention of crime, there would be little need to reform convicts, because without crime we would have no convicts. But how can we obtain such prevention? And where?

It can be accomplished in the home by people who are willing to fully assume their responsibility to be good partners in marriage and give proper supervision to their children. Parents can train their children to avoid crime, and they can avoid becoming embroiled in crime themselves. It is still true that if we train up a child in the way he should go, when he is old he will not depart from it. The increase in crime is a direct reflection of the failure of our homes.

Crime prevention can be achieved through building a spiritual atmosphere in the home, and by developing mutual confidence and respect between parents and children by parents living the gospel themselves and converting their children to its principles. In this way is developed the type of good character for which crime has no attraction.

No true Christian will rob a bank or assault another person, or become an embezzler or a fraud or a sex pervert. The answer to the crime problem is conversion to Christianity.

Such conversion must begin in the home, and it must begin with the parents. They must set the proper example. They must avoid dishonesty themselves; they must eliminate bickering in the home, criticism of each other, neglect of one another and neglect of children.

Parental failures have an uncomfortable way of being translated into the lives of their offspring, and thus are criminals born.

The answer to crime and to the reformation of criminals must be found in prevention, and that prevention can best begin with the adoption of the gospel into good family life. There is no other effective way.

WHERE DELINQUENCY STARTS

One of our stake presidents is a lawyer who has served for fourteen years as a prosecuting attorney. He feels that many of our people have become so affected by liberal philosophies that marriages are failing at a critical time in the lives of children, who thereupon frequently turn to the ways of the world.

These cases, he says, are the greatest heartbreaks of his profession. With that in mind, he sends us a copy of a letter written by a district judge to the legal publication known as *Judicature,* making the following plea:

"The public pays me thousands of dollars a year to help catch people in their erring ways, to point out their erring ways, and then to appropriately punish them. It makes me sick at heart — putting people in jail, taking money or property from one and giving it to another, deciding will contests and sending children to training schools.

"I grant from two to five divorces in a day, dividing up the children and/or property, knowing that 75 percent of juvenile delinquency is produced by broken homes. I send people to hospitals for mental illness or alcoholism, which usually causes or is caused by broken homes.

"And so I yearn and grope to try to stem this tide of human misery. I should be satisfied to just earn my pay and mind my own business, but I feel I am my brother's keeper whether in or out of court.

"We have a lot of nice 'do-gooders' who go to prayer meetings and pass out Bibles, but crime and delinquency and alcoholism and dope keep climbing. I think these 'do-gooders' need more to stick their necks out and take risks to stem this downward trend. We need prayer, but we also need courage and constructive action." (John W. Porter, Jr., District Court, Muskogee, Oklahoma.)

When the Lord said in the Doctrine and Covenants 68:25 that parents will be held accountable for their children's sins if the parents have failed to teach them properly, he stressed a great principle of child development.

Solomon said that if a child is properly taught he will seldom go astray when he is old.

Parents must remember that teaching must include example, and to provide a good example means to abolish selfishness, which is a prominent factor in divorce. Selfishness, rebellion, and a disregard for gospel principles are at the foundation of most divorces. It is no wonder that selfish parents afflict their children with conditions from which they seldom recover.

One of the great commandments teaches us to do to others as we would be done by. What parent has the right to cruelly thrust upon a child conditions which can force him into forbidden paths?

10.

CHILDREN AND YOUTH

YOUTH IN PERSPECTIVE

Youth movements which catch the headlines these days would almost make us think that certain youth of today are a brand of which the world has never heard before, a group demanding special attention, special treatment, special favors and advantages.

But is today's generation really so much different from the youth of the previous generations — the youth that we once were? Are they entitled to something better than was given to previous generations by way of rights and privileges? Should they be freed from the necessity to work, and never assume responsibility? Are there really any privileged classes?

After all, the youth of today are pretty much a cross section of the rest of humanity, very largely products of the environment about them. And it won't be too long before they outgrow their own youth and a new generation will take their places. What will the present youth think of their successors?

Elder Richard L. Evans once discussed this subject as follows:

"When is youth? Who is youth? Youth is a time we move through swiftly. Youth doesn't last very long — no more than any other age — and it should neither be an overprivileged nor an underprivileged segment of society — because at some time it is all of us — as other ages are.

"And to you who are young: it won't be long before you are older. And those who follow will ask what you have done with your life, as you ask this now of others.

"Remember, time is crowding you, right now — pushing you through your teens to your twenties, and then your thirties and forties — and so on — sooner than you suppose. And almost before you know it, you will be those who are older. And how will you look and feel, as you reach the other end?

"Youth isn't the permanent property of anyone. It is a corridor we pass through, without lingering very long. There is no stopping place for any of us. And all of us, young or old, should respect each other at all ages — for our strength is not in a society of segments, but in making the most of the whole length of life.

"Who is youth? When is youth? Well, it isn't a clique or a club in which we can claim perpetual place. It's a time of life we all go through, quite swiftly, quite soon.

"Oh, beloved young friends: Remember life is forever — but youth doesn't last very long. Live to make memories that will bless the whole length of your life."

A CHILD NEEDS LOVE

There is no substitute for mother-love. Every child needs it. Without it the child may suffer emotional problems and numerous other difficulties. Lack of it can produce a sad harvest for years in the future.

Mrs. Rita Chapman, Dallas, Texas, schoolteacher, writing in the Sunday supplement of the *Dallas Morning News,* makes a stirring plea in behalf of children who are deprived of their mothers' attention even during part of any day.

She is a homemaker, the mother of four children, and a professional teacher. She has taught elementary as well as preschool classes, and speaks from experience. Following are a few selected paragraphs from a lengthy but impressive article which she wrote:

"While vociferous proponents of women's liberation wave placards calling for more day-care centers, while women's magazines admonish us to get out of our homes and find fulfillment in careers, I seriously call for women who bear children to accept the responsibility of loving and shaping the children full-time, at least until they are school age. . . . I am totally convinced that once a woman has borne a child, she owes that child *herself* more than anything else the first five years of his life. . . .

"Let us not become so brainwashed as to believe that day-care centers are the panaceas for the homebound female. Let us not justify ourselves by saying, 'It's good for him. He's there with other children.' He's there with other children, but there's a good chance that he'll not be with another person *all day* who loves him — *really* loves him.

"I fear that raising emotion-starved and love-starved children can produce calloused, robotized adults — people who follow the group in straight lines and do exactly what everyone else is doing, because someone has said it is time.

"I fear for the working mother who is deluded to believe that some kind, patient woman will tend to her child's emotional needs until she can take over, that someone else will see that her child discovers he is unique, until she can pick him up at the end of the day — when she is perhaps so tired that the best he can hope to hear is, 'It's time to go to bed.'

"I fear for the future of the child whose hunger for love and recognition must be satisfied in large groups. I beg mothers to wake up, to experience the precious dawning of their child's life *with him*. Evening comes quickly — but in the evening may be too late."

CUDDLING CHILDREN

A child-care column conducted by Dr. William G. Crook in the *Houston* (Texas) *Post* carried the following letter from a reader:

"I am a child health instructor and the mother of a two-year-old daughter, and I'd like to comment on two problems I see frequently but cannot always handle tactfully.

"1. Too often, mothers use food as a means of giving love. When a baby cries or a child whines, a bottle or cookie is plunked into the youngster's mouth. This not only may make a child overweight but may begin a pattern of teaching the child that frustration is relieved by eating.

"2. Mothers seem to be holding their babies and toddlers less and less. Even infants in the newborn period are fed in their beds rather than being cuddled and held. After the baby gets home, the bottle may be propped.

"Researchers have shown a need for handling, cuddling and other close bodily contact if the infant is to grow and develop normally, both physically and emotionally. Parents should hold their babies more, not only for feeding but when playing games with them, reading to them, rocking them and so on."

To which Dr. Crook replied: "Your comments are excellent and very pertinent."

Explaining the power of motherhood, President David O. McKay said:

"Motherhood is the greatest potential influence either for good or ill in human life.

"The mother's image is the first that stamps itself on the unwritten page of the young child's mind. It is her caress that first awakens a sense of security; her kiss, the first realization of affection; her sympathy and tenderness, the first assurance that there is love in the world. . . .

"The ever-directing and restraining influence implanted during the first years of childhood linger with the child and permeate his thoughts and memory as distinctively as perfume clings to each particular flower." (*Gospel Ideals,* p. 452.)

The more a mother absents herself from the home, whether for social life or employment, the less influence she will have with her child.

The more a child is left with a "sitter" the more it will turn from the true mother to the foster one.

Is that the way it should go?

Writing in the same newspaper, Dr. Robert S. Mendelsohn commented on this point:

"In many day-care centers a child is brought up by strangers who may or may not have the same value system as the parents and who may or may not transfer to the child the same traditions and morality as that of their parents."

There is no substitute for good home life in the training of children, and there is no substitute in any home for a good mother who will fulfill the duties required of her to properly rear her little ones.

A child who grows up without good direction is indeed like the proverbial ship without a rudder.

THE CHILD VICTIM

British scientists are carrying on an extensive study of the children of smoking mothers, and are discovering that adverse effects stay with a child for as much as eleven years after birth. Their study thus far has stopped with the eleven-year-olds, but it may be projected even further to determine whether smoking mothers affect their children adversely for life.

A national sample of several thousand children has been followed from birth to their eleventh year. Both at the ages of seven and eleven significant physical and mental retardation has been found due to smoking during pregnancy.

It was interesting to note also that this deficit increases with the number of cigarettes smoked by the mother from the fourth month of pregnancy onward. Where mothers smoked as many as ten cigarettes a day, it was determined that a child was not only stunted in physical growth, but that in his school record he was as much as five months behind other students in his studies, particularly in reading and mathematics.

Details of the studies were published in the February 1974 issue of the *British Medical Journal*.

Issues of the same journal for 1973 carried similar reports, saying: "It is now widely accepted that maternal smoking in pregnancy is associated with both a reduction in birth weight and an increase in prenatal mortality."

CHILDREN'S RIGHTS

President J. Reuben Clark, Jr., was one of our greatest advocates of the rights of children, particularly their right to a proper birth and wholesome upbringing.

In one of his great general conference addresses he spoke of this matter as follows:

"I would like you to reflect upon the fact that our children came to us with spirits that did not ask us to bring them, but with spirits, through some operation of which I am not aware, that are assigned to us; and they come to us as our guests.

"We are responsible for the mortal tabernacling of that spirit, and I should like each and every Latter-day Saint to get that fact into his heart — that the child which is his or hers, comes at the invitation, virtually, of them who beget it, and then I would like you to reflect upon the responsibility which that brings home to each and every man and woman who is a parent.

"Yours is the responsibility to see that this tabernacled spirit loses no opportunity through you to prove his worthiness and righteousness in living through his second estate.

"Now the point that I wish particularly to emphasize is this — you parents cannot shift that responsibility to anyone else. It is yours; you cannot divest yourselves of it.

"You cannot give it to the state, and you ought not to give it to the state, for when the state takes over the direction, instruction, and rearing of its youth, then passes out, as the whole history of the world shows, the great principle of free agency, and not only that, but all the sacred principles of chastity and morality, with a host of other virtues which belong to a free society and are inherent in the governing principles of the kingdom of God.

"You cannot entrust your children, in the sense of having them take over your responsibility, to our schools. They cannot do your work. They may aid, and sometimes they may detract and defeat. I have referred before to pernicious doctrines which are appearing in our schools, not only political doctrines, which I would like you to note, but moral.

"The doctrine that the sex urge is like the urge for food and drink is born of Satan, and the man or woman who teaches it is Satan-inspired. Every effort you can make to prevent the spread of this doctrine you should make.

"You cannot entrust your children to society. That will never do. Society is too tolerant of wrong, too ignorant of matters of right living, too easy to betray and debauch.

"And lastly, the Church cannot take over the responsibility which is yours to train your children. The Church can aid, and should be the greatest aid; and we are derelict if we do not, as Church members and as Church organizations, provide that assistance.

"But beyond the Church — the Sunday Schools, and Young Women, the Primary, the Relief Society, and all the priesthood organizations — beyond that is the family, and it is our responsibility as parents to see to it that we fully perform our duties in this respect."

TEACHING OUR CHILDREN

There is a growing philosophy that children should not be taught denominational religion while they are small, but rather that they be allowed to make their own choice later in life.

More water has been poured on that very peculiar wheel by a New Jersey educator who herself has had much denominational instruction, but who would deny it to the rising generation, leaving youngsters to find their own way in religion as they grow up.

This lady has written a book in which she urges that children be taught only generalities about God, but no specifics and especially no doctrine. Her argument is that if a child is taught religion early in life he will only be confused by it, for such instruction might "set up mental blocks that will severely hinder his subsequent religious education."

Such is the wisdom of man. How different is the wisdom of God!

If children are left to their own devices with respect to religion, will they acquire any religion at all? With more than half the population of the nation never attending church, will parents in all these irreligious homes even raise the subject to their children?

Will children develop any desire for religion in a home of that kind? Never having been taught as children, will they worship an unknown God when they grow up? Will they be any different from their irreligious parents?

It was Solomon who taught that we should "train up a child in the way he should go, and when he is old he will not depart from it." Probably Solomon was at least as wise as the lady from New Jersey who thinks otherwise.

But even Solomon was not the final authority on this subject. The Almighty himself has discussed it, and his word is quite opposite to the deductions of certain child psychologists.

Supporting Solomon, the Lord goes even farther and says that parents must teach the gospel to their little ones in specifics, not generalities, or they will be held accountable for their failure to do so.

The Lord teaches that parents are to instruct their children about faith, repentance, baptism, remission of sins, prayer, the Sabbath, and the divinity of Christ. Are these not specifics? Are they not doctrine? This he gives as a law of heaven.

The Lord says that if parents fail in this regard, "the sin be upon the heads of the parents." (D&C 68:25.)

This may be news to authors and educators, but it is a sin to withhold from children specific instruction in regard to the doctrines of Christ. It might be news also to certain members of the Church, who may wish to change their ways and begin teaching these basics to their children.

TEACH CHILDREN TITHING

Most of our behavior patterns are formed in early childhood. It is then that habits are determined, standards are set and tastes developed. That is the time to teach the gospel to our little ones. The Lord commands it, even making it obligatory upon "all inhabitants of Zion." (D&C 68:26.)

One of the important things for children to learn is the principle of giving, of sharing, of overcoming selfishness which, if allowed to grow unchecked, will become their worst enemy. The Lord provided a divine method to help us in this matter. It is the principle of tithing.

The smallest child can be taught to share. He can be taught also that it is highly important that he learn to share with God, knowing that as we do so, we also share with our fellowmen.

The tithes of the Church are spent for the advancement of God's kingdom here on earth. Even little children can understand that they can do their part in helping the Lord with his work by sharing with him on a 10 percent basis any income that may be theirs.

And can they understand this 10 percent?

They have been taught already to say:

> "I know what tithing is,
> I'll tell you every time,
> Ten cents from a dollar,
> And a penny from a dime."

PITFALLS OF EARLY MARRIAGE

From the standpoint of statistics, it is safer to marry between the ages of twenty-three and twenty-five than at any other time. Fewer divorces occur among couples in that category than among others.

The highest rate of divorce comes among teenagers. As a rule, under twenty is a dangerous time to marry say the statisticians.

More than half of teenage marriages will end in divorce. For those who marry in their mid-teens the rate of divorce at times reaches the 90 percent bracket and frequently is found in the 70s and 80s.

And what are the principal causes of divorce among these youngsters? They are listed as:

1. Blind love.
2. Immaturity.
3. The rebound from premarital intimacies.

To be practical about it, we might truthfully say that immaturity covers all three points, and that it is the basic cause of both early marriage and early divorce.

Successful marriage requires maturity. It is in maturity that we really "do unto others as we would be done by," which is fundamental to happiness in the home.

Through maturity we balance our minds against our impulses, and thus avoid blind infatuations which good judgment would never condone.

And, certainly, it is through maturity also that we acquire the wisdom to avoid sinful practices which reproduce themselves in terms of conflict and deep remorse.

Immaturity is not limited to teenagers. Many are the adults who suffer from this malady and stumble into pitfalls which afflict those of all ages who have not reached the point where wisdom and purity govern their lives.

One of the saddest things about immaturity is the stubbornness with which it rejects wise advice and counseling as an individual forges his way toward disaster, headstrong and haughty, resenting every helpful hand.

How true are the words of Solomon:

"When wisdom entereth thine heart and knowledge is pleasant unto the soul, discretion shall preserve thee and understanding shall keep thee."

WHEN PARENTS WEEP

Parents weep when their children go astray because they know that only destruction comes of wickedness. And what parents can fail to weep when destruction comes to their own offspring?

The scriptures tell us that man is in the image of God. Some of the traits of man therefore also may be said to resemble those of the Lord. One of them is the sorrow parents feel over their wayward children.

Our Heavenly Father has such sorrow also. When the Lord showed Enoch the peoples of the world and the great wickedness of those people, the Almighty wept. And not only did the Lord himself weep, but the heavens wept also. And why? Because those people were children of God and they were treading the path to destruction, and were not repentant. The Lord sent prophets to warn them, but since they had their free agency — given them of the Lord — they could choose for themselves. And they chose evil rather than good.

The Lord understood the significance of that choice, for he knew the end of the course they were taking. He also knew that had they chosen the right, they would have had the possibility of becoming perfect even as he is perfect. In their blindness they rejected the Lord and the opportunity to become like him, and instead chose the opposite course which would make them like Lucifer.

As their Father, would not this make him weep? Seeing God weep made Ether wonder, so he asked the Lord how it was possible for him to weep, seeing that he had the riches of eternity. Then it was that the Lord explained:

"Unto thy brethren have I said, and also given commandment, that they should love one another, and that they should choose me, their Father; but behold, they are without affection, and they hate their own blood;

"And the fire of mine indignation is kindled against them, and in my hot displeasure will I send in the floods upon them [referring to the flood of Noah's day, Noah being the great-grandson of Enoch], for my fierce anger is kindled against them. . . .

"Wherefore, for this shall the heavens weep, yea, and all the workmanship of mine hands." (Moses 7:33, 34, 40.)

As do mortal parents, so evidently God also weeps over his errant children. But what joy he has when his children repent! And what joy we as mortal parents have when our loved ones leave the path of sin and begin to serve the Lord!

It is no wonder that the Lord said: "Remember the worth of souls is great in the sight of God; . . . And how great is his joy in the soul that repenteth!" (D&C 18:10-13.)

How important is repentance! How important it is that we have broken hearts and contrite spirits, and put the Lord first in our lives!

WHAT NEXT?

Isn't it time for adults to realize what they are doing to the rising generation of young people by making crime such a growing part of their lives?

We see crime in the movies and crime on TV. We read it on the front page of every paper. Some public officials and private citizens, bankers, lawyers and even the "little guys" participate in crime while the innocent bystanders stand aghast.

Now comes deception even in the Soap Box Derby. Read this and weep:

"Officials got suspicious when the winning car consistently jumped ahead of the pack at the start of various trial heats.

"It was these suspicions, officials said, that led them to make X-ray pictures of Gronen's racer, because derby rules strictly forbid the use of any force besides gravity to propel the downhill racers. In the meantime, Gronen won the 1973 All-American Soap Box Derby and a $7,500 scholarship.

"But the pictures revealed an electromagnet in the nose of his car, attached to coils and a battery in the rear. The revelation was the biggest scandal to hit the All-American Soap Box Derby. Gronen, of Boulder, Colorado, was disqualified.

"The X rays showed an activating switch operated by the boy's helmet. Officials said the magnet was turned on when the helmet of the driver touched the headrest of the racer.

"The cars line up on the edge of a ramp, held back by a heavy metal flap that falls forward and away from the racers, and allows them to roll downhill, over the metal plate. But when the metal flap holding Gronen's car fell forward, the magnet in his car could have caused it to stick to the plate as it fell, giving his car the boost needed to win so consistently."

The driver was a fourteen-year-old boy. No child of that age could or would have made a device such as was attached to his car.

What adult put him up to this deception?

What adult did the job on the car?

What adult was willing to sacrifice a boy's honor for a soap-box prize?

Children will hardly learn honesty while their adult teachers are so adept in the opposite direction.

SAVING OUR YOUTH

Only closer home and church ties with our young people can protect them from the invasion of degradation which is steadily mounting in almost every community.

Liquor consumption is on the rise, tobacco use has increased significantly during the past few years, drug abuse is still mounting, and immorality has reached epidemic proportions.

Public restrictions seem of little value in stopping the infiltration of the forces of destruction.

What can be done then?

We must turn more directly than ever to the home and the church.

In the days of the prophet Alma, he taught that the preaching of the gospel was more powerful even than the sword in putting down the enemies of righteousness. That same principle is true today. Nothing is as powerful as the gospel of Christ. It can defeat all enemies, it can solve all problems, it can heal all wounds — if it is only applied.

Dastardly as is the attack of evil forces, it can be turned back successfully by everyone who will take the gospel seriously, and truly live it and teach it.

If the gospel is taught properly in the home, both by word and by example, such good character may be developed there that no child will see any appeal in the major sins that afflict us.

Particularly if statistics are combined with gospel truth will the child receive strength. He will have the support of his faithful desire to live as the Savior lived, plus the strength of statistical and medical information which will show him the evil effects of immoral behavior and the use of drugs, tobacco and liquor.

The combination is unbeatable. There is nothing to compare with it. Faith in Christ and the facts of life used together will persuade anyone to live righteously.

What are parents to do then in the face of the public onslaught of wickedness? Strengthen the family by constantly obeying the gospel of Christ! If we sincerely teach it and live it, we then will learn as did Alma that the gospel is our strongest weapon against evil, and our greatest refuge in the storm.

We will find too that the gospel is the only means of finding true happiness in life, either here or hereafter.

THE NOBLE BIRTHRIGHT

Latter-day Saints often sing the great rallying song, "Carry On!" It points to the "youth of the noble birthright," and affirms in no uncertain language that:

> "Stalwart and brave we stand
>   On the rock our fathers planted
>   For us in this goodly land.
>   The rock of honor and virtue
>   Of faith in the living God.
>
> . . . .
>
>   O youth of the noble birthright
>   Carry on, Carry on, Carry on!"

The noble birthright — what is it? Is it worth the effort we are asked to put forth? Has it any real significance, any genuine relevance to today and its problems?

This noble birthright, what does it mean to us?

Long years ago the Savior spoke of our being born again, and thereby receiving a special kind of birthright. He said that if we keep his commandments he will accept us as his sons and daughters. And think what that means in terms of a birthright — to be adopted as the sons and daughters of Christ! It is well worth our most serious contemplation.

The Savior made our birthright even more understandable in modern revelation to the Prophet Joseph Smith. We can be joint heirs with him — heirs of "all that my Father hath." (D&C 84:38.)

In our finite condition we cannot understand the full extent of that promise, for God and his realm are infinite. But we can grasp it in part. If we are faithful, we can become "perfect, even as your Father which is in heaven is perfect." In fact we are commanded so to be. (Matthew 5:48.)

These are not idle words. "Heirs of God, and joint-heirs with Christ." This is the way the apostle Paul spoke of it. (Romans 8:17.)

To inherit the eternal blessings of God, to be classed as his children, to be taught how to become perfect as he is, to live with him in the hereafter in a glory so great that it is beyond our mortal perception, all this may be ours. And for now, we receive also the abundant life here in mortality.

Becoming the adopted children of Christ opens the door to all of these blessings. That is our birthright. It is noble; even more, it is divine! And it is ours to have if we will but serve him.

The youth of the Church — do they appreciate it? Most of them do. The vast majority are faithful. The new generation is wondrous to behold — clean, devoted, chaste, a rising "nation of priests," a peculiar people in the eyes of the world, but acknowledged by God as his own. They will not yield to worldliness. They will be true to Christ.

Hail to such youth! May they forever carry on.

11.

❦ HEALTH AND HAPPINESS

WE BARTER SURVIVAL!

How irresponsible will we allow ourselves to become? Shall we permit our appetites to completely destroy our sense of balance?

Are life, health and happiness not more precious than indulgence in suicidal drinking habits?

Intoxicating liquor has now qualified to become our national public enemy number one. Correct it, and watch the others disappear!

First, let us talk in terms of money, inasmuch as money seems to be such a controlling factor in modern life.

The United States Department of Health, Education and Welfare says that alcoholism and alcohol-related problems cost the United States economy $25 billion every year. It says that liquor costs America nearly $10 billion a year in lost production of goods and services alone; $8 billion in health and medical care; $6.5 billion in motor vehicle accidents; $640 million in alcohol program and research costs; half a billion in criminal justice proceedings; $2.2 billion in welfare payments; $4.5 billion in fire losses and $135 million in social service costs.

So reports the Associated Press.

In industry, alcoholism costs business houses $15 billion a year. The National Council on Alcoholism estimates that each problem drinker now employed costs his firm $3,000 a year in sick leave, accidents, lost production and, as *U.S. News & World Report* points out, bad judgment on the part of executives.

The HEW report to Congress, quoted above, also carried this paragraph:

"Cancers of the mouth, pharynx, larynx and esophagus and primary cancer of the liver appear to be definitely related to heavy alcohol intake."

It points out further that heavy smoking and heavy drinking together seem to be particularly implicated in mouth, pharynx and larynx cancer. Cancer of the pancreas is likewise associated with use of alcohol.

Drunkenness accounts for more than a third of the total arrests by police in the United States.

Alcohol plays a major role in twenty-eight thousand highway deaths each year in this country.

Use of alcohol shortens human life by from ten to twelve years.

Alcohol is a greater problem than drugs; for every heroin addict in America, there are at least fifteen hard-core alcoholics.

And who can measure the part liquor plays in broken homes, child abuse, divorce and poverty?

The Gallup Poll reports that the proportion of adults who drink — 68 percent — is now at its highest point in the thirty-five-year experience of that organization. Both drinking and highway accidents among youngsters over eighteen are skyrocketing.

Where is it all to end? Can the questionable "pleasure" of imbibing liquor and losing one's senses possibly compensate for the costs involved? Or is this a matter of sheer weakened character?

Can a government which spends $640 million a year in the treatment and prevention of alcoholism allow its citizens to barter away their health and prosperity to the tune of $25 billion a year?

At least private citizens should look to their own affairs and not allow liquor to be dominant in their lives. And Latter-day Saints can be ever more thankful for the Word of Wisdom!

LIQUOR OR FAMINE

America was properly shocked when the Associated Press quoted Harvard University nutritionist Dr. Jean Mayer as saying that in this nation every year we convert into alcoholic liquors enough grain to feed fifty million people in the starving countries.

Most alcohol is made from grain, Dr. Mayer pointed out, "and Americans drink enough beer and cocktails to feed fifty million people every year."

Dr. Mayer is director of the United Nations Task Force on Children's Nutrition. He said, "There is enough food in the world to keep people from starving in Africa and Asia, and America can make a major contribution by cutting down on its drinking habits."

Although he said he was not preaching prohibition, he did say that if Americans would reduce their volume of alcohol consumption they would be healthier and wealthier than they are today. In addition, they would save thousands of lives by providing food for the starving.

He spoke of the sacrifices Americans will have to make in order to assist the starving. But how much sacrifice would be involved if we eliminated alcoholic beverages?

In the United States there are ninety-five million drinkers of whom there are ten million confirmed alcoholics. Americans drink an average of 30.3 gallons of liquor, wine and beer every year.

A U.S. government report issued by the Department of Health, Education and Welfare recently said that alcoholic beverages drain the national economy of *fifteen billion dollars every year.* What a sacrifice it would be for Americans to be compelled to save that amount of money annually!

Alcohol is responsible for half the traffic deaths in America — about twenty-five thousand every year, to be more specific — and how much would it hurt this country to save that many people from death? It is remembered, of course, that some say we are suffering from overpopulation, but is killing people with automobiles the way to cure it?

There is also the matter of alcohol shortening the life of every alcoholic by from ten to twelve years. How much sacrifice would be involved in saving millions from this calamity? Or must we use this method also to save ourselves from this dreaded overpopulation?

There is still another consideration. Up to now the main thrust of our program to save the starving has been in the direction of birth control. Hence the public is warned to limit their families or we will all starve to death.

Now with this message from the Harvard professor, a vital new question is raised: To save the starving shall we give up our liquor or our babies?

So far the weight of current argument seems to favor contraceptives and abortions. To save the lives of starving hordes abroad, of course we will not consider giving up our liquor, but we are quite willing to destroy unborn life through the millions of abortions being performed upon women who do not want their own children.

What is worth most to us, our children or our liquor? It seems that appetite and pleasure still outweigh common sense among many people. But common sense still says we may best save the starving millions by proper farming methods and better distribution.

THE VERY FIRST DRINK

The very first drink you take of an alcoholic beverage damages your brain permanently. And brain cell destruction accumulates with every drink you take thereafter at any time or place.

Dr. Melvin H. Knisely reports this important medical discovery. He is a professor of anatomy at the Medical University of South Carolina in Charleston, and headed the team of research scientists.

When you take a drink of alcohol, Knisely says, the circulating red blood cells become agglutinated. This seriously interferes with blood circulation through the small arteries, capillaries, and veins. Agglutination means that the red blood cells become sticky and adhere together until the blood becomes, literally, a sludge.

The sludge resists passage of the blood through the capillaries and there is anoxia, absence of oxygen. As the level of alcohol increases, many small vessels become plugged and blood flow through them stops entirely.

Dr. Knisely says he once was a moderate social drinker, but he has quit. When he found the evidence of alcohol's effect on the brain, he says, he felt it was not rational for any human being to continue using it.

When brain neurons are deprived of oxygen, they stop their normal functioning. If complete oxygen deprivation persists for fifteen to twenty minutes, the damage is permanent and the nerve cell dies. Brain cells are irreplaceable. Thus, successive damage done to the brain accumulates throughout life.

THE LAST DRINK

Under the direction of the governor of the state of Texas, a publication on traffic safety is issued entitled *Texas Traffic Safety Report.*

One issue carried this statement:

"A $200,000 compensation recently was awarded by a California court to a three-year-old child whose parents were killed in an auto collision involving a drinking driver.

"The driver and his wife were also killed in the crash.

"The judgment was made against the bar that served the drunk driver his last drink. In making this ruling, the judge warned it also could apply to a private person, such as a party host who gives drinks to guests subsequently involved in a traffic crash."

THOSE STRONG DRINKS

When the Lord said that strong drinks are not good for the body he gave us a warning the full significance of which is only now beginning to dawn upon us.

How flippant many have been regarding the Word of Wisdom! How often it has been made the butt of jokes and snide remarks! But also how stern is the lesson coming home today in terms of billions of dollars of expense, broken homes, and industrial distress!

It is well known that alcoholism costs the nation over ten billion dollars a year due to absenteeism in industry, low production, poor judgment and inefficiency in general.

Forty million persons, as members of the families of the ten million alcoholics in America, are adversely affected by drink.

The situation in industry has reached a point where both unions and management are worried. Insurance companies, also affected, are joining with the companies they serve in fighting the menace.

Even the distillers are worried, and are telling people not to "drink too much" — as though even one drop were not too much.

Large companies are joining together to set up a program to fight the alcohol threat. Plans are being made to detect alcohol-prone employes. There is no immediate intention of discharging such workers, but the effort is toward rehabilitation, recovery and abstinence.

U.S. News & World Report has indicated that General Motors is carrying on a successful program in this regard, and says that it has more than a hundred committees working on the problem in the United States and Canada.

As a result, for example, in the Oldsmobile division alone there has been a 50 percent cut in lost man-hours, a 30 percent drop in sick leave and accident benefits, a 63 percent reduction in disciplinary actions, and an 82 percent cut in job-related accidents.

There has been an expansion in health insurance to cover treatment of alcoholics. One insurance company, the Kemper Group, has published a pamphlet entitled *Detour, Alcoholism Ahead* as a guide to detecting alcoholism.

General Electric has adopted an extensive program on the subject as has the St. Regis Company.

But while all of that goes on, the medical men of the nation regret that the government still considers alcohol as a food, in spite of all its addictive potential.

An issue of *Medical Tribune* declares that with few exceptions U.S. health officials "have turned their backs on disease-causing alcohol while they piously ply their attacks on medical therapies whose problems at worst are as pimples compared to the cancer of alcoholism."

Refusal of government agencies to act in the matter, the *Medical Tribune* says, "goes beyond the realm of comprehension if not decency."

Some day men may come to their senses and realize the truth of the Lord's declaration: "I have warned you, and fore-warn you, by giving unto you this word of wisdom by revelation — That inasmuch as any man drinketh wine or strong drink among you, behold it is not good." (D&C 89:4, 5.)

PARENTAL "PUSHERS"

Repeated newspaper accounts quoting government and medical experts have branded alcohol as our worst drug menace. There can be no doubt, considering cold statistics, that alcohol wrecks more lives than all the other drugs put together. And yet, what do we do about it?

Millions of dollars are spent in drug detection. Particularly at our borders a heroic work is being done in trapping clandestine agents of the drug traffic and seizing costly shipments of their enslaving products. This is as it should be.

But why do we seem to close our eyes to our wholesale alcohol addiction and the vast fortunes we lose because of it?

We exclaim tearfully over the thousands of people killed and maimed on our highways, but do very little about the fact that alcohol is to blame for at least half of those deaths.

What do we do to rid the highways of the one-in-every-fifty cars driven by a drunk? Why don't we do something about the countless numbers who take "one for the road" before they reach the highway and kill someone?

When it is known that liquor is our worst enemy on the road, isn't it incredible that we do not take adequate steps to control it? When it is known that liquor causes millions of dollars of losses to employers whose employes try to work under its influence or who absent themselves from the job, it is appalling that we do not control it.

And when it is so well known that liquor is associated with organized crime and prostitution, with divorces by the thousands, and with the suffering of millions of child victims of parental drinking, why do we fail to move in strength against it?

Canada is discovering the same thing that is well known in the United States concerning liquor. The Addiction Research Foundation of that nation reports that in terms of health and social costs, alcohol-related problems are responsible for more than 10 percent of all expenditures in general public hospitals, 15 percent in mental hospitals, 20 percent of all expenditures under the Family Benefits Act, and 30 percent of all costs of the Children's Aid Societies.

In 1971, Ontario taxpayers alone paid $89 million through the Ontario Hospital Insurance Plan for illnesses related to alcoholism; $17 million due to liquor through the mental hospital system, and another $20 million for family service and child-care programs in liquor-related cases.

The Associated Press recently reported that one reason campus riots have quieted down is that students have turned to alcohol from marijuana.

The same AP story said that of the twenty-four million alcoholics in the United States 25 percent are white collar, 30 percent blue collar and 45 percent professional — doctors, lawyers, judges and police.

Is liquor sacrosanct, that we dare not fight it as our worst social enemy? Are liquor interests so sacred that they must have inviolable protection? Must death, divorce, crime and immorality continue to be the price of appeasing our appetites or lining gangsters' pocketbooks with gold?

Probably one of the saddest things about this whole dirty mess is the fact that most young people learn to drink in their own homes. Most are given their first drinks by their own parents. Survey after survey has proven the truth of this.

If liquor, then, is our worst drug menace, who are the worst "pushers"? The parents? Who are creating the most addicts? Fathers and mothers?

The parents of the nation can control the evils of liquor if they will recognize alcohol for what it is, and take appropriate measures.

REFORMING ALCOHOLICS

Industry is finding that the best way to handle alcoholics is to reform them.

Some of the large corporations have abandoned the policy of discharging these unfortunate people in favor of a program of reformation whereby they save the man and all of the investment they made in him as they trained him for his position.

They have measured the expense of training new people to take the places of discharged alcoholics and have come to a realization that to reform the man, if he will cooperate, is much cheaper than to fire him and develop new talent to take his place.

There are ten million alcoholics in the United States, and they cost the nation $10 billion a year, counted in lost time, slowdowns in work, illness, mistakes of judgment, spoiled materials, domestic problems and the rest of the dismal picture.

Craftsmen trained by a company have achieved their skill only after years of apprenticeship, careful direction and literal "nursing" along by a supervisory staff. In cases of executives, the investment is still greater.

To lose its investment in a skilled man costs more than a company cares to afford. But when one individual case is multiplied by the number of alcoholics on a large payroll, the problem mounts to frightening proportions.

In most instances when alcoholics are discharged from their jobs, they usually degenerate further and cause severe social problems, often with divorce, neglected and abused children, juvenile delinquency, and various types of crime.

For this reason business is cooperating with government to retrieve the men who have lost themselves in drink. The federal government is spending about $200 million a year in this undertaking, plus what local governments and business organizations are putting into the program.

It is hoped that at least half of the liquor victims may be saved; but not all will be permanent cures. In fact, some U.S. senators are not sure we are gaining on the problem at all. Industry, however, feels differently. It is out to save both the man and the investment in his training, for strictly economic reasons. It's business with them.

How much better it would be if business and government saw the larger view and undertook a prevention program! What if they joined in a major educational effort to teach people that liquor is like poison, that it is completely destructive, both to health and jobs, and that whole families become the victims of one member's weakness.

Or better still, since the government legislates against drugs, and liquor creates our worst drug problem; and since our government legislates against poisons, false advertising of foods and illicit prescription rackets, why not legislate against liquor itself?

Must we drink? Must we have ten million alcoholics? Must their abuse cost the nation over $10 billion every year? Can we really afford such waste?

Why not develop enough common sense to abolish liquor as we abolish other poisons? But that is asking too much. We don't have that much courage, do we? Our appetites are stronger than our good judgment.

THAT LIQUOR TASTE

Liquor flavoring in food is being recommended more all the time. Almost every recipe you see in newspapers and magazines calls for it. Of course, it is perfectly obvious who promotes this kind of thing, because these promoters are trying to widen their market and sell more of their products.

They say in defense of their sales approach that liquor in cooked food will do no harm, for the alcohol evaporates and only the taste is left. But that is not the case. Hollis Waldon, of the Waldon Laboratories in California, makes this interesting observation:

"You may assume that since ethyl alcohol has a boiling point below that of water it would all boil off at temperatures well below 212° F. (100° C.) at standard pressure.

"This is not true. Ethyl alcohol and water form such a tight mixture that simple distillation will not completely separate the two compounds. For example, if we heat a mixture of alcohol and water we will find some water boiling off with the alcohol slightly above the boiling point of alcohol.

"As we continue to heat the mixture, we will find some alcohol is still present in the mixture at 200° F.

"This means that to completely cleanse our food from cooking alcohol, all of the food must be raised to a temperature above the boiling point of water.

"Many recipes do not require this thorough heating after alcohol is added and therefore the food remains contaminated."

An added difficulty is that as the brewers themselves say, the flavor or the taste of the liquor remains. This is one of the worst things about "liquor recipes" — the taste.

Who wants to deliberately give a taste for liquor to their family? Where will it end? Are we ready to take the consequence?

Are we not bright enough to recognize that putting liquor into food is just another means devised by the distillers to increase their sales? Will we be duped by such a device? And anyway, should Latter-day Saints have liquor in the home under any guise?

THE SUICIDE RATES

The *Los Angeles Times* has labeled alcohol as one of the world's major causes of suicide.

Not only does alcohol break up homes, kill thousands on the highways and lead to a variety of serious and often fatal diseases, it is now shown to be intimately related to suicide.

A fourth of all suicides are charged to alcohol by Mr. P. B. Anderson, staff writer for the *Los Angeles Times*. But, he says, especially high suicide rates exist among female alcoholics and male homosexual alcoholics.

The close relationship of suicide and alcohol abuse was discussed by physicians attending a meeting of the American Association of Suicidology held in Los Angeles.

Alcohol abuse is a slow form of suicide, Dr. Robert E. Litman, chairman of the Los Angeles Suicide Prevention Center, said. "Most people contemplating suicide don't really want to kill themselves," Dr. Litman said. "They want to get rid of the pain of loneliness or depression."

Women alcoholics often kill themselves after a divorce or when their adolescent children create problems and the woman believes she has failed as a parent, according to Dr. Basil Clyman, head of the Los Angeles County-USC Medical Center's detoxification unit.

"The same problems affect men," Dr. Clyman said, "but women are more susceptible. It is easier for a man to seek reassurance from his work or from new friends."

The gay male has similar depressions.

"Both groups can have no sense of purpose — and that is what life is all about."

He said that women increasingly are consuming alcohol. He added that the severe depression that usually precedes self-destruction is "almost certainly" caused by a chemical imbalance in the brain.

As was once said about tobacco, so we might equally well say of alcohol — if spinach were known to be as dangerous as liquor, it would have been banned by government edict long ago.

TEEN GIRL SMOKERS

Statistics indicate that more and more adults are quitting smoking, but that an increasing number of teenagers are taking up the habit, especially girls.

It is well accepted that this increase is largely an indication that smoking is a status symbol, an evidence that "all we like sheep" try to do what "everyone else" does because it is popular.

Popularity and status at that age seem to be more important than health or good sense. As one authority said, "When they grow up they will learn to quit, even though they don't want to be confused by facts at this time in their lives."

In any case, let us review some of the facts provided by the American Cancer Society. Statistics show that one in every four teenage girls using tobacco also uses marijuana regularly.

In the United States there are nearly three million teenage girls who smoke regularly and of those 87 percent are also drinkers, compared with only 42 percent of the nonsmoking girls.

The smoking girls have a higher rate of immorality than do nonsmokers, the figures being 31 percent against only 8 percent for nonsmokers. Only 3 percent of nontobacco-smoking girls use marijuana.

Half a million more teenage girls smoke now than was the case in 1969.

The Cancer Society figures indicate that the proportion of thirteen- to seventeen-year-old girls who smoke rose from 22 percent in 1969 to 27 percent today. Worse than that, the 1969 poll indicated that only 10 percent of all girl smokers used a pack a day, but that now 40 percent use a pack a day.

The federal HEW figures provided by the National Clearinghouse for Smoking and Health show that teenage girls are now smoking almost as heavily as boys.

Most of the girl smokers come from families with less than ten thousand dollars annual income, and where fathers were high school drop-outs.

A third of the smoking girls have parental approval.

These girls have a strong acceptance of illegal drugs.

Smoking is more and more becoming known as a means of slowly committing suicide. But when girls smoke, and subsequently become mothers, the effect upon their children is likewise most unfortunate.

Would they care to read these frightening statistics? Or do they prefer to wait and learn the hard way?

HOW COFFEE HURTS

In 1973 *Town and Country* magazine carried an illuminating article about the harmful effects of coffee. The conclusion of the study as explained in that article was: don't drink it.

After explaining that coffee causes low blood sugar levels, loss of vitamin B, skin problems, ulcers, headaches, some heart trouble, upsets insulin mechanisms, and that it goes hand in hand with cigarettes and its dangers, the article concludes:

"What perhaps is the worst thing about coffee that can be deduced from various sources — from nutrition experts to heart specialists — is that, like most stimulants, coffee too can become habitual.

"More and more is required for stimulation, for the daily "pickup" or lift. And this is where the habit becomes pernicious, for while it provides a feeling of well-being, it is merely whipping up the endocrine glands (most usually the adrenal glands) and is thus masking fatigue and other underlying problems that may range from vitamin deficiency to faulty metabolism to emotional depression."

It is interesting that Dr. Oglesby Paul, professor of medicine at Northwestern University School of Medicine, said this about coffee in his book, *Postgraduate Medicine:*

"In a study of 1,718 men — those who drank five or more cups of coffee a day — it was shown that these men had an increased incidence of angina pectoris and myocardial infarction."

Dr. Paul indicated that caffeine has a significant effect on blood lipides (fats and fat-like substances normally present in the body) and carbohydrate metabolism.

He said that several studies have demonstrated an association between the coffee habit and an increased incidence of coronary disease.

Gradually we learn from science what we first heard years ago from the prophets. But how many coffee drinkers are willing to believe either?

COFFEE AND YOUR HEART

A number of publications have carried results of a study on the relationship of heart trouble and coffee drinking. The following is from *Science News Letter* (104:4):

"A heart attack is an acute obstruction of the blood supply to the heart. Late last year, Hershel Jick and his colleagues at Boston University Medical Center reported that 276 patients who had had acute heart attacks had drunk more coffee than 1,104 control patients with other diseases (*SN:* 1/6/73, p. 10.)

"They now have more findings, reported in the July 12 *New England Journal of Medicine,* to strengthen the link between coffee drinking and heart attacks.

"This time they surveyed 12,759 hospitalized patients, including 440 who had had acute heart attacks. Again they found a strong correlation between coffee drinking and heart attacks.

"If people drank one to five cups of coffee a day, their risk of having a heart attack was 60 percent higher than those who drank none. If they drank six or more cups a day, the risks were 120 percent higher than those who drank none."

COFFEE AND UNBORN BABES

Studies made in Utah and Idaho among eight hundred women indicate that coffee consumed during the first three months of pregnancy can harm or even kill an unborn child.

This startling statement appeared in the *National Inquirer* and reported results of a research study completed at the University of Illinois.

It was reported by Paul S. Weathersbee, graduate research assistant at the university. He said that he is certain that there is a definite relationship between the consumption of coffee and pregnancy problems. If six cups a day were consumed by a pregnant woman during the first three months, they could bring serious and possibly fatal results, said Weathersbee.

In a group of fourteen women drinking seven or more cups of coffee a day, thirteen had pregnancies which ended in miscarriage, fetal death or stillbirth.

The *National Inquirer* quoted Dr. Michael F. Jacobsen co-director of the Center for Science in the Public Interest, Washington, D. C., as saying that earlier studies also show that caffeine causes birth defects and reduces fertility in animals. He has requested the Department of Health, Education and Welfare to conduct further studies, and to warn the public about the potential dangers of caffeine.

QUASHING THE KILLERS

Cancer is the number two cause of death in the United States, and completely banning cigarettes would be the most effective way to reduce the death rate from that disease, it is declared by Dr. Brian MacMahon of the Harvard University School of Public Health.

"No single known measure would lengthen the life or improve the health of the American population more than eliminating cigarette smoking," the learned doctor said in a special report issued to the Associated Press on the risks of death by cancer.

Almost simultaneously, the U.S. Department of Health, Education and Welfare issued a report attacking both tobacco and alcohol as vicious enemies of good health and major causes of death. This report was issued by Dr. Theodore Cooper, of HEW, who pointed out that both alcohol and tobacco contribute heavily to heart disease, cancer, and respiratory troubles.

He said that "death and disability from those factors are preventable primarily by changes in individual behavior." That was a soft way of saying: Stop smoking and drinking!

A third report, this one on alcohol alone, came at the same time. It was a state medical release issued by the California Office on Alcoholism, Health and Welfare.

It said flatly that since the drinking age limit was reduced, young drinkers under eighteen have caused nearly all of the recent increase in arrests for alcohol-related offenses. While adult arrests in such cases increased only 1 percent in a year, such arrests among juveniles jumped 22 percent. And juvenile drunk driving arrests in California went up 100 percent in one year.

Americans are reputedly an intelligent people. If they really are, why do they not eradicate these killers — alcohol and tobacco?

We outlaw food coloring before it is definitely known if it contains any cancer-causing agents, we take suspected pesticides off the market, and we scream to high heaven about smoke arising from the stacks of our smelters.

On the other hand, we do virtually nothing to protect the nation against these two vicious killers, both of them identified as such and both of them chalking up tens of thousands of deaths each year.

The inconsistency of it all is appalling.

THE WORD OF WISDOM

How important is it for Church members — and particularly officers and teachers — to live the Word of Wisdom?

The Prophet Joseph Smith, back in 1834, gave us the answer which became a statement of policy all Latter-day Saints should accept.

This statement by the Prophet is in accord with the action of the High Council of the Church shortly after its organization in February, 1834. At one of the earliest meetings of this council over which the Presidency of the Church presided, this question came up:

". . . Whether disobedience to the Word of Wisdom was a transgression sufficient to deprive an official member from holding office in the Church, after having it sufficiently taught him?" After a free and full discussion, Joseph Smith the Prophet gave the following decision which was unanimously accepted by the council:

"No official member in this Church is worthy to hold an office after having the Word of Wisdom properly taught him; and he, the official member, neglecting to comply with and obey it." (*Teachings of the Prophet Joseph Smith,* p. 117.)

Although the Word of Wisdom is a basic statement regarding health, it has a vital bearing on our spirituality. It is the "word and will of the Lord" and as such cannot be violated without damage to our spirituality.

Do we not resist the word and will of the Lord when we refuse to live this law? And if we are in defiance of God's word, can we claim to be exemplars in his kingdom? Can we even pray in full faith? Can we expect the companionship of his Spirit?

Without the protection of the Holy Spirit, we open ourselves to all the fiery darts of the adversary, as described by the apostle Paul (Ephesians 6:16), and in this day do we not need the full protection of the whole armor of God?